Walks with Walser

Carl Seelig

WALKS WITH WALSER

Translated by Anne Posten

A NEW DIRECTIONS PAPERBOOK ORIGINAL

New Directions gratefully acknowledges the support of Pro Helvetia, Swiss Arts Council.

swiss arts council

prohelvetia

Originally published in German as *Wanderungen mit Robert Walser*

Manufactured in the United States of America
New Directions Books are printed on acid-free paper
First published as New Directions Paperbook 1373 in 2017
Design by Erik Rieselbach

Library of Congress Cataloging-in-Publication Data
Names: Seelig, Carl, 1894–1962, author. | Posten, Anne, translator.
Title: Walks with Walser / Carl Seelig ; Translated by Anne Posten.
Other titles: Wanderungen mit Robert Walser. English
Description: New York : New Directions Publishing Corporation, 2017.
Identifiers: LCCN 2016039676 | ISBN 9780811221399 (alk. paper)
Subjects: LCSH: Walser, Robert, 1878–1956. | Authors, Swiss—20th century—Anecdotes.
Classification: LCC PT2647.A64 Z813 2017 | DDC 838/.91209—dc23
LC record available at https://lccn.loc.gov/2016039676

10 9 8 7 6 5 4 3 2

New Directions Books are published for James Laughlin
by New Directions Publishing Corporation
80 Eighth Avenue, New York 10011

How ill at ease we feel in the present world
with its great wheeled machines,
if we don't consecrate our personal existence
to nobler ends.

> —*Jacob Burckhardt*
> (from a letter to Albert Brenner,
> October 17, 1855)

July 26, 1936

OUR RELATIONSHIP BEGAN with the exchange of a few sober letters: short, matter-of-fact questions and answers. I knew that Robert Walser had been admitted to the Waldau psychiatric clinic near Bern at the beginning of 1929, and that since July 1933 he had been under care at the Sanatorium of Appenzell in Herisau. I felt the need to do something for his work and for him personally. Of all the contemporary writers in Switzerland he seemed to me the most peculiar. He agreed to let me visit him. And so, early one Sunday morning I drove from Zürich to St. Gallen, strolled through the city, and listened to a sermon on the Parable of the Talents in the collegiate church. Bells in the church were ringing when I arrived in Herisau. I announced my arrival to Dr. Otto Hinrichsen, the head doctor of the asylum, who granted me permission to take a walk with Robert.

The fifty-eight-year-old writer comes out of a nearby building, accompanied by an attendant. I am astonished by his appearance: a round, childlike face that looked as if it had been struck by lightning, with a hint of red in the cheeks, blue eyes, and a short golden mustache. His hair already graying at the temples; his collar frayed and tie a little crooked; teeth not in the best condition. As Dr. Hinrichsen moves to fasten the top button of Robert's vest, he fends him off: "No, it must remain open!" He speaks in melodic *Bärndütsch*, the same Bernese dialect he had spoken in his youth in Biel. After the doctor's somewhat abrupt departure, we set out for the Herisau train station and continue on toward St. Gallen. It is a hot summer day. On our way we encounter many churchgoers, who greet us pleasantly. Robert's older sister Lisa had warned me that her brother was uncommonly mistrustful. What am I to do? I'm silent. He is silent. Silence is the narrow path on which we approach each other. Our heads burning in the sun, we ramble through the landscape—the hilly, tranquil landscape of woods and meadows. Often Robert stops to light a Maryland-brand cigarette, and holds it, snuffling, under his nose.

Lunch in Löchlibad. The first signs of a thaw over beer and blood-red Berneck wine. Robert tells me that before the turn of the century he had worked in Zürich at the Swiss Credit Institute and the Cantonal Bank. Only for a month or two at a time, though, just enough to free him to write again. One cannot serve two masters at once. It was during this time that he wrote his first book, *Fritz Kocher's Essays*, which was published in 1904 by Insel Verlag with eleven drawings by his brother Karl. He was never paid for the book, and when it sat around in the bookshops, it soon ended up being sold off for cheap. His remove from literary cliques ultimately had severe financial repercussions, but the cultishness that is common practice in many places is simply repugnant to him. It degrades writers, turns them into mere bootblacks. Yes, he can feel it—his time is past. But that does not bother him. As one approaches sixty, one has to begin thinking of another existence. He had written his books just as a farmer sows and mows, grafts, feeds the cattle and mucks their stalls. Out of a sense of duty, and in order to earn a little something to eat. "For me it was work like any other."

He tells me that his most productive period was the seven years he spent in Berlin and the following seven in Biel. No one had harried him, no one had controlled him; everything could grow as peacefully as apples on an apple tree. The years following the First World War were a shameful time for most writers. Literature had taken a vitriolic, spiteful turn. But literature ought to radiate love—it should be comforting. Hatred should never be allowed to become a driving force. Hatred is unproductive. It was then, amid the orgies of gloom, that his artistic decline had begun ... The literary prizes were distributed to false prophets and pedants. Well and good, there was nothing he could do about it. But he swore that till the day he died he would bow to no one. Cliquishness and nepotism contained the seeds of their own destruction anyway.

Throughout this conversation: admiring comments about Dostoevsky's *The Idiot*, Eichendorff's *Memoirs of a Good-for-Nothing*, and the bold, masculine poetry of Gottfried Keller. Rilke on the other hand he deems bedtime reading for old maids. Jeremias Gotthelf's two *Uli* books are dear to his heart, but much of the rest of his work is too coarse, blustering, and moralistic for Robert's taste.

January 3, 1937

A WALK THROUGH St. Gallen and Speicher to Trogen, a place already familiar to me from my time in the cantonal school there. Lunch at the Schäfli Inn. In honor of my maternal forebears, who for centuries kept vineyards in the Rhine Valley village of

Buchberg, I order a bottle of rich Buchberger wine. A blaring radio provides an unrequested encore: a Swabian comedy.

Up Gäbris in the afternoon, in a melancholy, snowy mood. As a young cadet lieutenant there I'd cut a foolish figure, with my hefty sword borrowed from the village doctor. Biting though intermittent east wind. Robert without an overcoat. On our return by train: his face now glows from within like a lit torch. Deep, painful lines from the bridge of his nose to his conspicuously red, fleshy mouth. The little pebbles of the train platform at St. Gallen sparkle. Robert has tears in his eyes. A fierce, hurried handshake. Extracts from our conversation: his sojourn in Zürich lasted, with interruptions, from the fall of 1896 until early 1903. First he had a place on the Zürichberg, then on Spiegelgasse and in the Schipfe district, then in Aussersihl. He spent seven years (from 1906 to 1913) in Berlin, and another seven in Biel. It had often occurred to him that the number seven periodically recurred in his life.

In Berlin-Charlottenburg he lived first in a two-room apartment with his brother Karl, and then alone. Eventually the publisher Bruno Cassirer refused to continue to support him financially. For the next two years a good-hearted rich lady took care of him. After her death in 1913 he had no choice but to return to his homeland. For a long time afterward he still thought often of the quiet beauty of the Märkisch woods. In Bern, where he lived for about eight years, beginning in 1921, the staunch traditionalism of the place was beneficial to his literary production. The temptations of drink and a life of ease, on the other hand, had a negative effect. "Sometimes in Bern I was like a man possessed. I chased poetic motifs like a hunter his prey. My promenades through the city and long strolls through the surrounding area proved most fruitful; later at home I would then commit them to paper. Any good work, no matter how minor, requires artistic inspiration. It is clear that for me the business of writing can only blossom in freedom. Morning and night were the best times to work. The hours between noon and evening had a stultifying effect on me. During that period my best customer was the *Prager Presse*, which was financed by the Czech government; the *feuilleton* editor there, Otto Pick, would print anything I sent, even poems, which came back from other newspapers like boomerangs. I often worked for *Simplicissimus* as well. The editor repeatedly rejected my pieces, however, because he didn't find them funny enough. But what he took he paid for well. At least fifty marcs per story—a small fortune for my pocket."

I ask: "Perhaps the milieu and residents of the asylum will provide material for a novel someday?" Robert: "I should hardly think so. In any case, I would be unable to develop it as long as I remain here. Dr. Hinrichsen went so far as to provide me with a room for writing, but I simply sit there as if nailed to my seat, writing nothing. Perhaps if I were to live in freedom for two or three years outside of the asylum the great breakthrough would come …" I: "How much would you need to live freely as a writer?" Robert, after a moment's consideration: "Eighteen hundred francs per year, at a guess." "No more?" "No, that would suffice. How often in my youth did I have to make do with less! One can live quite well without material things. In any case, I could never commit myself to a newspaper or publisher. I don't like making promises that I can't keep. Everything must simply grow out of me without being forced."

Later: "If I could turn back the clock to my thirtieth year, I wouldn't write so aimlessly, like some happy-go-lucky romantic, eccentric and untroubled. One should never reject society; one must live in it and either fight for or against it. That is the error of my novels. They are too whimsical and too reflexive, their composition often sloppy. I flouted artistic principles and improvised as I pleased. I would have liked to cut seventy or eighty pages from *The Tanners* for the new edition; now I think it wrong to publically cast such intimate judgments on one's own siblings."

I ask: "I read your *Jakob von Gunten* recently with the greatest pleasure. Where was it actually written?" Robert: "In Berlin. It is a poetic fantasy, for the most part. Rather daring, don't you think? Of the longer books it is also my favorite." After a pause: "Often I find the less plot a writer needs, and the more restrained his setting, the more significant his talent. I am immediately wary of writers who excel at plot and claim practically the whole world for their characters. Everyday things are beautiful and rich enough that we can coax poetic sparks from them."

A conversation about the playwright August von Kotzebue, whose grace and ease in society Robert admires. He recalls that Kotzebue was exiled to Siberia for a year at the beginning of the nineteenth century, and that he wrote a two-volume memoir about the experience. He had met a dramatic end as well, at the hand of the hyperpatriotic youth league member Karl Ludwig Sand. As a critic of Goethe and Schiller, Kotzebue had acted as a reactionary stumbling block. Robert does not believe progress possible in Swiss literature as long as it remains mired in provincialism. It must become more urbane and cosmopolitan, leaving behind narrow, earth-burrowing peasant concerns. He praises Uli Bräker, the Poor Man of Toggenburg, and his essays on Shakespeare. What a contrast between the ideals of contemporary writers and those of Gottfried Keller, whose poem "A beautiful legend wanders" Robert recites from beginning to end. Keller's *Green Henry*, he says, is a charming, educational book that will remain well worth reading for generations to come. "An attendant at the sanatorium recently tried to force Stifter's *Witiko* on me. But I conveyed to her that I had no interest in such a corpulent novel. Stifter's nature studies are enough for me—those incomparably deep observations, with human beings placed so harmoniously among them. But what do you say to Thomas Mann's potbelly of a Joseph trilogy? How can anyone dare to take material from the Bible and stuff it up that way?"

On revolutions: "It is absurd to try to stage an uprising outside of the city. Without the cities, one cannot possess the heart of the people. All successful revolutions have come from cities. And so I consider it a certainty that the regime will ultimately be victorious in the Spanish Civil War." And: "The Wilhelmine era tolerated the extravagant behavior of artists; it accommodated misfits. Yes, it positively indulged eccentricity. But artists too must learn to conform. They must not allow themselves to become clowns."

June 27, 1937

FROM THE FOGGY crucible of St. Gallen, in a mail van to Rehetobel. From there on foot to Heiden and to the village of Thal, home of my maternal forebears, which lies nestled in the valley as if in a green cradle. After lunch, up through the vineyards of the Buchberg to the pub Zum Steinernen Tisch, which offers a wide view over the region around Lake Constance. Later to the idyllic hamlet of Buchen through a fierce storm, over the Rorschacherberg, and on to Rorschach. Return by train.

"Do you know what my downfall has been? Listen carefully! All the dear, sweet people who think they have the right to criticize me and order me around are fanatical admirers of Hermann Hesse. They don't trust me. For them it is either/or: 'Either you write like Hesse, or you are and always will be a failure.' They are extremists in their judgment. They have no faith in my work. And that's the reason I have ended up in this asylum ... I simply lacked a halo, and that is the only way to be successful in literature. Any aura of heroism, martyrdom, or the like and the ladder to success rises before you ... I am seen as rather merciless, which I am. And thus no one takes me very seriously."

Incidental remarks: "When newspapers smile, mankind weeps."

"Nature does not need to make an effort to be meaningful. It simply is."

"How many Nobel laureates will already be long since forgotten while Jeremias Gotthelf lives on in all his comfortability! As long as there is a canton of Bern, there will be a Jeremias Gotthelf."

"The writer C.F.W.—he looks like an actor in a farce."

"Happiness is not good material for writers. It is too self-sufficient. It needs no commentary. It can roll itself into a ball and sleep like a hedgehog. Song, tragedy, and comedy, on the other hand—they are full of explosive power. One must only be able to set them off at the right time. Then they rise into the sky like rockets and illuminate everything around them."

December 20, 1937

LIGHT SNOW. ROBERT stands at the train station without an overcoat, but carrying an umbrella, rolled up like a sausage. He doesn't seem to notice the cold. We stroll through St. Gallen and turn into the restaurant Gilge, where we are the only guests. Robert speaks for a long time of the comely cross-eyed waitress who ran her hand over his back. "We should have stayed there!"

When I say over lunch at Marktplatz that the waitress serving us now is much prettier than the one from earlier—she has such nice legs—he says that is not the point. He considers the entirety of a person, and above all, her nature.

In a clothes shop we try several suits for Robert. The manager takes him for my father. The ready-made clothes do not suit him, however, his back is too round. He wants something "for a farmer, in any case nothing conspicuous." Since the measuring and fussing and tailoring make him increasingly nervous and his head is beginning to turn red, we flee together without buying anything.

Dimly lit Bavarian beer hall. Strong beer. He likes it here. He lights one "Parisienne" cigarette after another, never stopping. With dry irony he asks me if I cut a good deal on his anthology, *Big Small World*, published by Verlag Rentsch. Praises Wieland and Lessing, while finding Matthias Claudius too naive. Says: "I was never jealous of the classic writers, but rather of the second-rate ones, particularly Wilhelm Raabe and Theodor Storm. For I could have done that sort of thing too, writing pleasant bourgeois stories as they did. Raabe's perfect comfortability I find downright vexing." I: "So are you also jealous of Gottfried Keller?" Robert, laughing: "Him? But he was from Zürich!"

I tell him that he is to be honored by the Committee for the Promotion of Bernese Literature. This pleases him.

April 15, 1938

ROBERT WALSER'S SIXTIETH birthday. From what I know of him, congratulations would only turn him sour. Our reunion commences in the Herisau train station restaurant with cheese pie and pints, and Robert remarks: "I haven't had a sip of cheer since New Year's!" We start off at a sharp tempo for Lichtensteig, the main town in Toggenburg, thirty kilometers away. We take narrow, lonely pathways, where we meet only a few churchgoers. Robert stops often to admire the charm of a hilltop, the sturdiness of a tavern, the blue of the paschal day, the peaceful seclusion of a stretch of landscape, or a greenish-brown clearing. He sneezes constantly, having come down with the flu the week before. Degersheim, a tidy little village. Over a hill to Lichtensteig, which we reach four hours later. Hearty lunch near the town square; afterward, a pastry shop where we each buy a sack of *Biberli* cookies to take home. Return by train to Herisau. Beer at the station restaurant, and then a crisp Neuchâtel wine at the Eidgenössiches Kreuz, where Robert feels particularly at ease. He praises the delightful day and makes plans for our next meeting. He thinks a walk to Wil would be worthwhile. At the station, I finally congratulate him on his birthday. He shakes my hand several times, runs after my train, and waves until it disappears around the corner.

From our conversations: In Berlin Robert trained for one month at a servant school. He describes the deferential refinement of many servants. He was hired by the valet of a count to work at a castle on a hill in Upper Silesia, high above a village. Robert was made to clean the halls, polish silver spoons, beat carpets, and serve in a tailcoat as "Monsieur Robert." He stayed there for half a year. He depicted the school for servants later in *Jakob von Gunten*, where he recast the milieu as a boy's academy. "But in the long run my Swiss clumsiness made me ill suited for a servant." The castle once received a sensational visitor: Baroness Elisabeth von Heyking, the author of the then-popular book *The Letters Which Never Reached Him*.

After the servant episode, his brother Karl, the painter, introduced him to the publishers Samuel Fischer and Bruno Cassirer in Berlin; at that time Karl had just gained notice for some theatrical decorations he'd made for Max Reinhardt's productions of *Tales of Hoffmann* and *Carmen*. Karl often painted with Max Liebermann in Holland and on the Baltic. Bruno Cassirer encouraged Robert to write a novel. The result was *The Tanners*, which Cassirer, however, didn't particularly care for. One critic claimed that the novel was nothing more than a collection of footnotes.

The conversation turns to Maximilian Harden, for whose magazine *Die Zukunft* Robert had occasionally written. He praises Harden's aristocratic nature and his talent for capturing the age in his brilliant articles. Robert rates him even above Ludwig Börne, whose melodious language he also admires. He names Heine the most important German-language journalist: his mischievous nature is perfect for the profession. He describes Harden's downfall, which logically began with Germany's defeat in the First World War.

Robert worked for a few weeks in Zürich in the offices of the Escher-Wyss machine factory, and spent some time as a servant to an elegant Jewish lady. However, he liked Biel the most. "I had little to do with the Bielers themselves. I chatted with the foreigners who came to the Hotel Blaues Kreuz, where I lived in a garret apartment. Room No. 27 cost twenty francs, full room and board was ninety francs. There were chambermaids, all sorts of lovely female creatures with a slight French air that I found charming." I ask: "Then why did you leave Biel?" Robert: "I was very poor at the time. And the motifs and details that I drew from Biel and its surroundings were gradually beginning to run dry. At that point my younger sister Fanny wrote that she knew of a position for me in Bern, at the cantonal archives. I couldn't say no. Unfortunately after half a year I fell out with the director on account of an impertinent remark. He dismissed me and I picked up the trade of writing once again. Under the influence of that powerful, vital city I began to write less like a shepherd boy; my writing became more manly and international than it had been in Biel, where I had used a prim style. The result was that—enticed by the name of the Swiss capital—many queries and contracts came for me from foreign newspapers. It was imperative to find new motifs and ideas, but all the brooding took a toll on my health. During my last years in Bern I was plagued by wild dreams—thunder, shouting, a choking in my throat, hallucinatory voices—so that I often awoke screaming. Once in the middle of the night I walked from Bern to Thun, where I arrived at six in the morning. At midday I was at the top of the Niesen, where I blithely devoured a piece of bread and a can of sardines. By evening I was in Thun again, and at midnight in Bern; all on foot, of course. Another time I walked from Bern to Geneva and back, spending the night in Geneva. One of my earliest travelogues was about the Greifensee, which Josef Viktor Widmann published in *Bund*. Even back then I found it damnably difficult to write a good travelogue."

"Literature must be like a beautiful suit that flatters one into buying it."

"Peter Altenberg: a dear little wienerwurst. But I could never grace him with the title of 'writer.'"

"The Austrians would never have fallen for the Nazis if they had put some smart, charming madam in charge of the country. Everyone would have huddled around her, even Hitler and Mussolini. Just think of Queen Victoria or of the Dutch queens! Diplomats are always happy to serve women. There are no such charming flatterers as the female Austrians!"

"I prefer not to read my contemporaries as long as my position remains that of an invalid. This preserves the most appropriate distance."

"What use is an artist's talent if he lacks love?"

"Jeremias Gotthelf: With him I feel exactly like the woman in Heinrich Pestalozzi's novel *Lienhard and Gertrud* who says: 'The priest druv me outta the church!'"

He tells, half in exasperation, half in amusement, of a certain Frau A., whom he has known since childhood; now she is the wife of a well-to-do postal clerk. She's taking him for a ride, on the one hand bombarding him with chocolate bonbons, and on the other taunting him with impertinent letters: "I still cannot really take you seriously!" In this she has an ally in Thomas Mann, who once in a letter unceremoniously reduced Walser to a "clever child."

April 23, 1939

ROBERT EXPRESSES A desire to go "over Germany way," to Meersburg. But the cool, overcast spring morning is actually made for a walk, he says. Would a hike to Wil be all right with me? Why not! A harmonious mood matters more to me than the direction.

Robert has his umbrella with him as usual; his hat grows ever shabbier. The band is in tatters. Yet he does not want a new one. Everything new is distasteful to him. Nor will he allow his problematic teeth to be straightened or fixed. All this is burdensome to him; I hardly dare to speak of such things, although his favorite sister Lisa has asked me to see to them.

We make the way from Herisau to Wil in three and a half hours, chatting the whole time. We feel as if we're on roller skates, we trot along so easily. Sometimes Robert points out a particularly beautiful meadow, a cloudscape, stately baroque houses. He does not object to my photographing him. I'm flabbergasted. It makes him happy and cheerful to have covered the twenty-six kilometers so quickly, with only vermouth for "fuel." In the first pub there are two wrinkly old ladies and a young one. They study the radio program and, when we get up to leave, come over to our table to shake our hands.

Wil. We eat at Im Hof; we are tremendously hungry and stop for a bite at one pub after another. Five, in total. Robert suggests that we not take the train back to Gossau now, at half past three, but that we leave in two hours. He wants to spend as much time together today as possible. He now frequently looks me in the eye; the distance and dryness that he likes to barricade himself with has given way to a quiet trustfulness. His train to Herisau leaves two minutes after mine. When my train begins to move, he bows twice, deeply and very seriously. Is he thinking of "Monsieur Robert," the castle servant? Now I too bow twice and call out: "Next time over Germany way!" at which he nods brightly and waves his hat.

At the beginning of our walk Robert told me the following story of a trial: A lawyer in London was accused of killing his wife. His amiable and gracious nature so impressed the judge, however, that a favorable verdict seemed likely. The accused, on the other hand, had a different opinion. He decided to flee to the United States with his pretty secretary, on whose behalf he had killed his wife. He was arrested on board the ship. Misjudgment of the psychological situation cost the lawyer his life, for his attempt to flee raised the judge's suspicions. The floor of the kitchen was torn up and the dismembered corpse was discovered below. Thus the murderer lost himself his life. If he had continued to play the amiable man, he would most likely have been acquitted. The moral: you may perhaps fool others, but you can never fool yourself for long.

"In 1913 when I returned to Biel from Berlin with a hundred francs to my name, I considered it advisable to behave as inconspicuously as possible. There was really nothing to crow over anyway. I took solitary walks day and night; in between I carried on the business of being a writer. Finally, when I had grazed up all the motifs like a cow its meadow, I cleared off to Bern. There too, things went well at first. But imagine my horror when one day I received a letter from the *feuilleton* editors of the *Berliner Tageblatt* advising me to write nothing for half a year! I was devastated. Yes, it was true, I had written myself dry. Burned out like an oven. In fact I pushed myself to write, despite this warning. But I labored over foolish trifles. It has always been only what grows peacefully out of me, what is somehow experienced, that turns out well. I made a few bumbling attempts to take my own life. But I was unable even to make a proper noose. In the end things got so bad that my sister Lisa brought me to the Waldau Sanatorium. At the gate I asked her: 'Are we doing the right thing?' Her silence said enough. What choice did I have but to enter?"

"It is absurd and brutal to expect me to scribble away even in the asylum. The only basis on which a writer can produce is freedom. As long as this condition remains unmet, I will refuse to write ever again. Simply providing me with a room, paper, and a pen will not do." I: "I have the impression that you don't really want freedom at all!" Robert: "No one is offering it to me. So that means waiting." I: "Would you really want to leave the asylum?" Robert (hesitating): "One could try!" I: "Where would you most like to live, then?" Robert: "In Biel, Bern, or Zürich—it makes no difference! Life can be charming anywhere." I: "Would you really start writing again?" Robert: "There is only one thing to do with this question: not answer it."

In the last months Robert read with pleasure Johann Gottfried Seume's adventure-filled autobiography, *A Stroll to Syracuse*, and Gottfried Keller's *A Village Romeo and Juliet*, as well as the novella *Goethe and Therese* by the Bavarian nature poet Martin Greif. He says: "An artist must enchant his audience or disquiet it. He must make people cry or laugh." I tell him that a Swiss schoolmaster has written a novel set partly in a Paris brothel. Robert's reaction: "Dreadful, what impotent hacks can sink to!" On the state: "It strikes me as philistine to pester the government with moralistic demands. The primary duty of the state is to be strong and vigilant. Morality must remain an individual affair."

I: "Shall we have supper somewhere?" Robert: "What for? Liver and veal with mushroom sauce cannot cheer me! Let us drink instead! That's what does me good. I can still eat as often as I like. Every day. But drinking? That I can do only with you!"

September 10, 1940

ROBERT'S HAIR GROWS whiter and whiter; little snow-white clusters sprout at the nape of his neck. We fortify ourselves first with beer and two pieces of cheese pie. I suggest we hike to Teufen, the township his family comes from. He agrees and asks: "On the road?" I: "Yes, if you prefer it. But it's pouring, Herr Walser!" Robert: "So much the better! One cannot always walk in the light."

We set out, passing Hundwil and Stein. Rain now pours down as if from watering cans. At one point we stop under the shelter of a bus stop, where an old woman who has never ridden in a car or train is sitting on a bench. I chat with her. Robert stands mutely next to me and smokes one of the "Parisienne" cigarettes that I brought him.

On the way we talk about the Reinharts, a family of art patrons in Winterthur. Alluding to this, Robert later remarks: "You look so Reinhartly today!" I: "How so?" Robert: "So lordshiply, full of the airs of nobility. A bit uncanny!" I: "This afternoon I have to attend the funeral of a relative in St. Gallen." Robert, dryly: "Indeed."

His memory of events from the distant past is striking. He remembers dozens of names and particulars from the lives of Frederick the Great, Napoleon, Goethe, Gottfried Keller, and others. He considers it no coincidence that Keller chose to spend his seventieth birthday in the *Urschweiz*. Instinctively, on that day he wanted to be close to the heart of his nation—in the old, original part of Switzerland.

For attempts to write in the vernacular, he, Robert Walser, has little use: "I deliberately never wrote in dialect. I always found it an unseemly way of ingratiating oneself with the masses. An artist must keep his distance. The masses must have respect for him. Any person whose talent is based on trying to write more like a man of the people than others must be a real dolt. Writers should feel fundamentally obligated to think and act nobly and to strive for greatness." When our conversation turns toward Walter Hasenclever, who committed suicide in France, Robert remarks: One cannot rail against the power of the father with impunity. Even in Berlin I understood Hasenclever's play *The Son* as an affront to all fathers. The desire to fight eternal laws is a sign of intellectual immaturity. One runs the risk that the laws will have their revenge."

Robert admires the unfailing instinct for national interest that dictators have. It is a natural law that they have to be ruthless to survive: "Since dictators almost always rise from the lower classes of society, they know precisely what the people long for. By fulfilling their own wishes, they also fulfill those of the people. The people love it when someone acts on their behalf, when someone is fatherly, by turns loving and stern. In this way one can even win the people over to war."

"Have you noticed that each publisher thrives only in a particular era? The workshops of Frobenius and Froschauer in the Middle Ages; Cotta with the rise of the bourgeoisie, masters Cassirer in the prewar *dulci jubilo*, Sami Fischer in the young Germany throwing off the fetters of imperial rule, the adventurous Ernst Rowohlt in the postwar gamble. Each brings just the right atmosphere to the enterprise to reap a juicy profit."

At the asylum he has been asked to write a poem for the seventieth birthday of the head doctor, Dr. Otto Hinrichsen. "But how could I? That sort of thing should be written by the person himself, as J. V. Widmann does—preferably in an ironic, joking way. Look at Goethe and Mörike! From them one can really learn gentle self-mockery."

We reach Teufen in three hours and settle down in a butcher shop for veal in mushroom cream sauce, beans, and *Rösti* potatoes. Robert prefers a Fendant to the wines from Eastern Switzerland. Over black coffee we talk of the asylum. I: "Have you ever noticed that it is primarily unmarried men and women who have mental breakdowns? Perhaps repressed sensuality has an adverse effect on the mind? Think of Hölderlin, Nietzsche, or Heinrich Leuthold!" Robert, hesitating: "I never thought of that. But perhaps you're right!... Without love, man is lost."

March 21, 1941

A RIDE ON the Appenzell railway to Gais, whose noble Baroque architecture Robert finds charming. Lunch at the Krone. We are served by a tall waitress: slim, with a young face but very gray hair. "She has a breast like a swan!" Robert whispers to me. A walk to Teufen, the ancestral home of the Walser family. According to the town records, Robert's great-grandfather, Dr. Johann Jakob Walser—a wealthy doctor and senator who had twelve children with his wife, Katharina Eugster from Speicher—was a citizen of Teufen and lived there from 1770 to 1849. The town register goes back no further. It's snowing while we're having a look at the village; later the sky clears. Robert has no time for family history, however. He shakes the topic off with distaste. Instead he tells me of the novelist and poet Max Dauthendey, who was a disciple of the cosmopolitan Walt Whitman. "I tried to visit him in Munich once. But I found only his wife, who told me that her husband happened to be in Würzburg. I therefore took this as an opportunity to set off in that direction, in light sandals and without a collar. I covered the distance in a little over ten hours. That was the fastest walk I ever took. My feet were full of blisters when I arrived.

"In Munich I spent quite a lot of time with Frank Wedekind. He asked me where I had gotten such a lovely, large-checked suit. I said, 'I bought it in Biel for thirty francs.'" Wedekind had fond memories of Aarau and Lenzburg, which inspired his first successful play, *Spring Awakening*. The Swiss found Wedekind too uncomfortable, however: too fiendish, too vagabond. Their hatred of such an *enfant terrible* was indescribable. Robert remembers a bit of dialogue from Wedekind that goes: "How will he recognize your mother at the train station?" And the answer: "By her despair!" The Swiss rationalists did not have the faintest understanding of such things.

"Whether you believe it or not: One day Bruno Cassirer suggested I write novellas like Gottfried Keller. I roared with laughter. It's a true misfortune for a writer not to gain recognition right away with his first book, as was the case for me. Then every publisher considers himself entitled to give suggestions about what will bring the quickest success. Such seductive insinuations have ruined many a weaker character."

"Regarding music: it should be reserved for the upper classes. In large quantities it has a stultifying effect on the masses. Nowadays music is served up in every *pissoir*. But art must remain a gift of grace, toward which the simple people gaze with yearning. It must not descend to the sewer. That is false, and appallingly vulgar. Sincerity, charm, and elegance are indispensible in art ... Personally, in ordinary circumstances I do not desire music at all. I prefer a friendly conversation. But when I was in love with two waitresses in Bern, I longed for music and chased after it like a man possessed."

July 20, 1941

ROBERT STANDS, WAVING, at the Herisau train station under an overcast sky, and steps into my compartment without a ticket: "Do you mind if we continue on? I have no money, however!" I: "Of course! We shall simply buy a ticket onboard!" He wears a clean collar, but his tie is quite askew. During our walk his collar gradually loses its shape. I notice a large bald spot on the right side of the back of his head. The doctor has apparently already pointed it out to him as well.

We ride to Urnäsch. Just before leaving the village I ask him if we should stop for a bite. "No, better not. We've hit our stride— we have to take advantage of it!" Few other walkers, several cyclists. Robert is remarkably cheery and talkative; several times he uses the informal with me, quite casually. I notice that his mouth is like that of a fish gasping for breath as it is pulled on land with a fishing rod: very red and often open, the bottom lip somewhat bulging. The tip of his nose curves slightly upward.

Across from the Jakobsbad spa there is a cloister-like, baroque building, most likely a nursing home. I: "Shall we look in?" Robert: "Such things are much prettier from the outside. One need not investigate every secret. I have maintained this all my life. Is it not lovely that in our existence so much remains strange and unknown, as if behind ivy-covered walls? It gives life an unspeakable allure, which is increasingly disappearing. It is brutal, the way everything is coveted and claimed nowadays."

Our conversation is varied as we hike toward Appenzell, where we indulge in beer and nut crescents at Krone. Robert does not want to linger, however. And so we walk onward to Gais, our pace always brisk. There, at a different Krone, we consume a grandiose meal with a bottle of Beaujolais. Afterward a pastry shop, and on foot via Bühler to St. Gallen. Fierce rain on the way. We hole up in the Bayrische Bierhalle, where we slowly dry out. Robert tells me that an old friend of mine from the cantonal school, Egon Z., has been admitted to his ward, where he's had agitated discussions with the doctors about a rich factory owner's daughter, whom he believed he could marry. He's become intractable and defiant, Robert says, also a bit haughty, but otherwise interesting, stimulating, and bright. "He plays up his masculinity and believes he can impress others with it. But he comes off like a schoolmaster. This role suits him like a rain-soaked skirt on a clothes hanger." Egon had said to his next-door neighbor in the asylum: "Look at Walser! He can still even concentrate when he reads!" When I tell Robert that my old schoolmate's first name is "Egon," he pauses in delight and laughs: "Wonderful, wonderful—this noble name! It says so much. It positively demands a life worthy of a novel. Does one not have to become a Stendhalian with such a name? For this Egon Z., all women are simply the trapeze that allows him to fly higher. His misfortune, however, is that women will not stoop to his level, since he is still half peasant."

Robert continues: "For the past few weeks there has also been a postman in our ward, a well-to-do man who now walks around the same table day in and day out and behaves rather indecently." I: "I imagine you prefer not to have neighbors of that sort?" Robert: "Why not? Such crackpots are quite welcome. They bring color to the gray of asylum life."

He informs me of the death of the asylum's physician, Dr. Otto Hinrichsen, originally Otto Hinnerk from Rostock. He took over the cantonal sanatorium in Herisau in 1923. A nice obituary by the new head doctor, Dr. H. O. Pfister, had appeared in a newspaper. To Robert, however, Hinrichsen had seemed like a cross between a courtier and a circus performer. He could be charming, particularly at Christmas, but he was also very moody. When his comedy *Garden of Love* was produced in the Stadttheater St. Gallen, he had surprised Robert with the question: "Have you heard about my triumph, Walser?" I: "And how did you reply?" Robert: "I said nothing, as is my custom in such cases. Restraint is the only weapon I possess, and it befits my humble status. I found it unseemly, however, that a seventy-year-old in an exalted position should draw attention to himself with comedic romances. Once the doctor also gave me his play *The Venerable Timborius*. But I did not read it. He had to die without ever knowing my opinion.

"Another time he sat down next to me and asked 'What is that you're reading?' To which I answered: 'Heinrich Zschokke.' Dr. Hinrichsen: 'Can one still really read that stuff?' To that too, I was silent. Can one still read Zschokke! He's a subtle writer, full of noble sentiments. Look at the story 'The Solider in Jura,' *The Goldmaker's Village*, or his *Look at the Self*, wherein he describes his encounters with Kleist and Pestalozzi! What a genial man! But his Swiss novellas I often have to choke down like dry wood. There he seems false—he did come from Magdeburg, after all. Writing them was simply a polite gesture, but one cannot make palatable literature from politeness alone."

On the subject of productivity: "It is not good for an artist to expend himself too much in his youth, or he will be fallow before his time. Gottfried Keller, C. F. Meyer, and Theodor Fontane all saved their creative powers for old age! And certainly not to their detriment." I: "How was it with you?" Robert: "During the last months in Bern I felt like my noggin was nailed shut. I simply could not find a motif. Incidentally, Gottfried Keller perhaps experienced something similar when he took the position of Official Secretary of Zürich. Always knocking about the same place can lead to impotence." I: "But your observation does not hold for many artists, for example Jeremias Gotthelf, who spent his whole life in the same atmosphere." Robert, who knows my enthusiasm for Gotthelf, and wants to rile me a bit: "I have studied Gotthelf closely. I believe I can say that you are incorrect. In fact it was just the same for him. But he had a big mouth. He simply couldn't hold his tongue, the bonehead. He always had to go around correcting everyone until they could no longer stand the sight of him. This realization finally broke his will to live. I do not mean to say that he was wrong. He was an important writer, a powerful preacher who had the best of intentions toward his countrymen. But one cannot take a position against one's own country with impunity. The Bernese must have seen it as a betrayal that he so often preached down to them in front of others. For it was really the Germans who read him most … I will always marvel at Goethe's social instinct and his genius for conjuring up just the right project for each period of his life. In that he has no equal. When he was tired of writing poetry, he refreshed himself in the realms of geology and botany, with ministerial or theatrical activities. He was always discovering new sources of rejuvenation."

On Nietzsche: "He took revenge for the fact that no woman ever loved him. He became unloving himself. How many philosophical systems are nothing but revenge for pleasures foregone!"

In a conversation about revolutionaries: "Do you remember how the French generals ended up killing each other out of suspicion, jealousy, and ambition, paving the way for Napoleon and a king? It could go the same way for Hitler and Stalin. Perhaps Russia will dig them both a grave ... Georg Büchner depicted this tragedy of revolutionaries brilliantly in *Danton's Death*."

Of himself: "Wherever I've lived there have always been conspiracies to keep out vermin like myself. Anything that does not fit into one's own world is always grandly and haughtily repelled. I never dared to push my way in. I wouldn't even have had the courage to take a peek into that world. And so I lived my own life on the periphery of bourgeois existence, and was that not a good thing? Does my world not also have the right to exist, even if it seems like a poorer world, a powerless world?"

"You ask where I did military service? In Fusilier Battalion 25, Third Company, and in Militia Battalion 134. I always got along with my comrades. But the officers would often say: 'Walser, yer a lazy wretch!' It never bothered me much."

May 11, 1942

AN UNFORGETTABLE TRIP up Säntis! The sky gray like the hide of a donkey. I apologize to Robert for not having brought friendlier weather. He says: "Is human life always sunny? Is it not light and shadow that give life meaning?" Puffing on a cheroot, he steps into my compartment. We ride toward Urnäsch and talk first of Herisau, the beautiful old part of which cannot be seen from the train. A market town, Herisau is the beehive of Appenzell. There is no more populous town in either the Inner or Outer Rhodes. But the honor of hosting the Swiss barracks in Breitfeld only fell to the Herisaurians after a bitter fight at the Trogen cantonal assembly of 1862, to the detriment of Teufen. Fourteen votes were necessary before an official result could be declared. Robert tells me that when construction began the ground was boggy, leading to a comical debate in the Grand Council. One person suggested—and Robert mimicked his heavy accent—"that the barracks be built with three stories instead of two from the first. So when the first story slips into the ground there'll still be two left!" Herisau now often teems not only with recruits, but also with patients, who bring their ailments to the natural healers and dentists here.

Chatting like this, we come to Urnäsch, which lies in a chive-green valley. Here in 1673 the last bear in Switzerland was killed, a nearly two-hundred-pounder. As we cross the village in the yellow-orange mail van, which has to force its way through a stubborn crowd of Braunvieh cattle that are being herded up the alp by three dairymen smoking silver-studded "Lindauerli" pipes and an Appenzell mountain dog, who runs to and fro like a nervous sergeant major. We are the only passengers on the suspension railway, which has run since 1935 from the Schwägalp to the summit of Säntis. We feel like a weather balloon as we pass the fifty-one-meter-high pylon and sail into the heights, into the thick fog that transforms the whole Säntis massif into a steaming washhouse. Unfortunately the 2100-meter distance and 1200-meter vertical change is behind us in ten minutes. We find the ride wonderfully dramatic. Pieces of ice and snow begin to crash into the windows like a wild hailstorm. When we press our noses to the cold glass, we see snow-covered limestone crags looming toward us like threatening cyclopean breasts. Impressions of Hodlerian power. It seems incomprehensible to us that there was so much protest against the building of this railway. Are there not still dozens of other approaches to the summit of Säntis, where at worst ill-mannered walkers disturb the more serious hikers? Why shouldn't old and sickly people also have the opportunity to enjoy the Alpstein massif? These are the questions we ask ourselves as we enjoy the dramatic selection of weather that unfurls before us.

We use the two-hour stop to visit the Swiss weather keeper. An icy northeast wind badgers us as we trudge along, without hat and coat, through knee-deep snow toward the little stone house where the Bernese Ernst Hostettler has lived with his wife for the last eleven years, walled in by winter for nine months of the year with no one but themselves for company. Just once a year they take a three-week holiday and travel to visit their son in Zürich, to see the elegant shops and the Circus Knie. But then the difficulty breathing, the sweltering heat of the city, and all the motors begin to bother them, and they travel on to the Bernese uplands to hike through the mountains. "One must break with everything one has become accustomed to as a lowland person in order to bear the loneliness up here," the weather keeper says, as we thaw out in his parlor. He grumbles a bit about the many mountaineers and photographers whose intrusions often sour his work. This work occupies about sixteen hours a day. The first report is transmitted at half past six Central European Time to the army weather station. Five reports follow, exchanged between the army, the Dübendorf airfield, and the Federal Office of Meteorology in Zürich. The last observations proceed at half past nine at night, but they are only for synoptic evaluation. All of this requires complicated instruments and precise knowledge of the forty-five types of clouds in the international weather codex, which is broken down into five hundred numerals, so that the reports have practical value. Robert sits quietly on the sofa during all these explanations. But as we trudge upward through the snow to the inn, he says: "Now instead of a view of the mountains we've had an equally interesting view into the lives of two people!"

Inside the tavern we learn that it has only been a hundred years since Säntis was opened to international tourism. In 1846 the first mountain hut was constructed; two decades later the first little inn; the Swiss weather station in 1887, where in 1922 the gruesome murder and robbery of the Haas couple took place. Another tragedy occurred on July 5, 1832, when Colonel Anton Buchwalder, an engineer of the Swiss trigonometrical survey, originally from Delsberg, was struck by lightning while constructing a panorama. The assistant standing next to him was killed, while the left side of Buchwalder's body was paralyzed. Nonetheless he walked or crawled to Toggenburg to warn the townspeople.

And so we do not lack for conversation topics as, after the ride up Säntis, we walk on from Urnäsch to Appenzell. On the way we see several women with fine, almost Mediterranean features sitting inside the narrow windows of the wooden houses, embroidering monograms. Robert says that they must work hard from morning until deep into the night to earn their day's wages of four francs. In Herisau I suggest: "Let us drink another glass of wine to toast the Appenzellerland!" "Don't mind if I do!" he replies, tipping his old felt hat politely.

January 28, 1943

A RATHER ARDUOUS hike over the icy road from Herisau to St. Gallen, where we warm ourselves in the station restaurant with coffee and cigarettes. Robert is amazed that we need ration cards for a portion of cheese. We take the train through empty streets to Heiligkreuz, the last stop. The conductor cheerfully tells us the way to Lake Constance. We trot off, turning left past the church, and through the dusky woods to the St. Peter and Paul game park, whose geese, stags, and deer emerge out of the thick fog like characters from a fairy tale. Robert is delighted. By the time we reach the game park restaurant we have completely forgotten the conductor's complicated directions, and so we turn down some street and ask two or three people for Lake Constance. They are amused that we want to walk so far. At an inn whose sign reads "Zur Sonne" we order vermouth and hot cheese pie. It tastes magnificent. Afterward the chubby waitress tells us we're not far from the tram station where we disembarked an hour and a half ago. And so we turn back and start down the big military road toward Rorschach, which we reach in two hours, just after twelve. The main street is quiet as a graveyard. Robert's collar and tie have come undone during the hike. I advise him to stick them in his coat pocket. But instead he disappears into a bathroom in the harbor to tidy himself up. When he emerges, his collar and tie are completely askew. I tell him that women will like him regardless. He laughs, reassured. We stroll unhurriedly around the city. Robert stops in awe before many shop windows and houses. The elegant, baroque style of Rorschach appeals to him. He can hardly tear himself away. Finally we decide to eat at the Traube, a pub attached to a butcher shop. But in the restaurant we find only the proprietress and a blonde girl sitting before a bowl of corn, who says: "You can't eat here!" We see the stove standing cold in the kitchen. We study the menus of several other restaurants before winding up at Post, which was recommended to me by a toll keeper. We drink red Buchberger wine and order the daily special, which really is quite good: calf's liver with mashed potatoes, beans, and peas. We clean our plates completely, and then continue chatting in a pastry shop over black coffee. We return to St. Gallen and to a bookshop, where I buy Gogol's novella *The Overcoat* for a friend. Coatless and carrying his rolled-up umbrella, Robert leads me like a mountain sprite through the narrow alleys, as though following a scent. I don't want to disturb him, and follow like a lamb. When we reach the city theater I realize that he's looking for the dim Bayrische Bierhalle we had been to before. He obviously feels at home here, and begins to talk of himself unprompted—a rare occurrence. At the market we buy oranges, which he loves, and then lukewarm chestnuts from a loud woman with a lame right arm. Farewell drink at the station restaurant. Several times Robert says: "That was a delightful day—don't you think? How about Bischofszell next time?" Once again I notice that his blood-red, fleshy lips look like the mouth of a fish dying of thirst as it's pulled out of water. As if gasping for breath.

Of his youth: "From Biel, where I went to primary and secondary school, and then had a three-year apprenticeship at the Cantonal Bank, I went to Basel, in spring 1895, to work as a clerk for the bank and shipping company von Speyr & Co., but only stayed a quarter of a year. My brother Karl, who worked at the time for an ornamental painter in Stuttgart, advised me to come join him. I therefore answered an advertisement placed by a publishing company—the Deutsche Verlags-Anstalt—and was offered a position in the advertising department. I stayed until autumn 1896. Then I wandered to Zürich, where I found employment first at an insurance company, then at a credit institute. In between I was often unemployed, which is to say that as soon I had rustled together a bit of money, I handed in my notice so that I could write undisturbed. Anyone who wants to do something properly must give himself to it fully, in my experience. Writing, too, requires all of one's strength. Yes, it downright bleeds one dry. Writing on the side, as an arabesque, so to speak, rarely yields anything lasting. During that time, there on Spiegelgasse, where Lenin lived and Georg Büchner died, parts of *Fritz Kocher's Essays* came to be, including the chapter about the painter. Another part was written on Trittligasse, on the right-hand side as you climb the steps from Oberdorf. When I was in the direst need, I copied out mountains of addresses at the unemployment office.

"Do you know why I didn't make it as a writer? I want to tell you: I possessed too little social instinct. I performed too little for society's sake. Certainly, that's how it was! Now I see that completely. I allowed myself to act far too much as I pleased. Yes, it's true, I had the disposition to become a kind of tramp, and I hardly resisted it. This subjectivity vexed readers of *The Tanners*. In their opinion the writer should not get lost in subjectivity. They consider it arrogant to take one's ego so seriously. How wrong then is the writer who imagines the world is interested in his private affairs!

"Even my literary debut gave them the impression that I was bored by good bourgeois citizens, that I found them somehow not quite good enough. They never forgot that. And so for them I remained always a zero, a ne'er-do-well. I should have mixed a little love and sorrow into my books, a little solemnity and approbation—and a little lofty romanticism, as Herman Hesse did in *Peter Camenzind* and in *Knulp*. Even my brother Karl reproached me for that from time to time, in his tender, roundabout way.

"Yes, I'll tell you frankly: in Berlin I was fond of hanging about in vulgar pubs and cabarets. That was when I lived with Kari and a cat named Muschi, in the studio where he painted his Czech girlfriend with the Russian wolfhound, but not me. Up there I flouted the world. I was happy in my poverty and lived like a dancer without a care in the world. In those days I also boozed prodigiously. And so in the end I became rather impossible, and it was pure luck that I found my way back to my sweet sister Lisa in Biel. I never would have trusted myself to go to Zürich with such a reputation.

"Once in Berlin the Swabian playwright Karl Vollmöller, who was born in the same year as I and in those days was Max Reinhardt's protégé, said to me, with unbelievable insolence: 'Robert Walser, you began as a clerk and a clerk you'll always be!' And then he intrigued against me at Insel Verlag when they published *Fritz Kocher* ... The end result: now he is completely forgotten, and so am I!

"I reread *Green Henry* in the asylum. It pulled me into its arms just as always. Imagine: Gottfried Keller, that cheeky devil, sat on the supervisory board of the Bürgholzi asylum in Zürich! Heinrich Leuthold's eyes must have popped out of his head when he saw Keller going around on an inspection. He must have nearly sunk into the ground with shame. It's an example of what can be accomplished through self-discipline, and what through dissipation.

"Now I long to return neither to Biel nor Bern. Here in Eastern Switzerland it is also quite lovely. Don't you think? I find it delightful, in fact. You saw how warm and cheerful everyone was to us today! I require nothing more. In the asylum I have the quiet I need. It is time for young people to make the noise. It suits me now to disappear, as inconspicuously as possible. Was this day not beautiful? We're no idolaters of the sun. We love the fog and the dusky woods as well. I will think often of the silver-gray of Lake Constance, the fairy-tale woods in the park, and the sleepy, aristocratic little town of Rorschach."

April 15, 1943

ROBERT'S SIXTY-FIFTH BIRTHDAY!

Long meeting with Dr. H. O. Pfister, the head doctor of the asylum, about Robert's physical condition. In mid-March he had to be brought to the district hospital in Herisau for enteroparesis; the doctors suspected a cancerous tumor in the lower large intestine, which could only be remedied through a somewhat risky operation. Robert took the diagnosis as if it had nothing to do with him. On the other hand, as much as the doctors and his two sisters might coax Robert to consent to the operation, they were met with an obstinate "No." Since the enteroparesis resolved after a few days in the hospital, Robert was returned to the asylum, where his condition improved markedly. Now he has begun to help the nurses clean the ward in the mornings again, in order to sort lentils, beans, and chestnuts during the regular afternoon work times, or to glue together paper bags. He strives to get through as tall a stack as he can and becomes grumpy when disturbed. In his free time he likes to read yellowed illustrated magazines or old books. He has never showed any inclination toward artistic creation, Dr. Pfister says. He harbors a deep-seated suspicion of the doctors, nurses, and his fellow patients, which he nonetheless skillfully tries to hide behind ceremonial politeness. Those who do not keep their distance risk being rudely snarled at.

I bring Robert a few birthday gifts, which he coolly sets aside. We've hardly left the grounds of the asylum when he asks me what I was doing so long with Dr. Pfister. I answer that we talked about doctors of our mutual acquaintance in Zürich. This explanation seems to reassure him, but the morning's walk to Degersheim and Mogelsberg in Untertoggenburg nonetheless remains rather monosyllabic. He doesn't respond to my gentle inquiries about the operation. I therefore turn away from the subject immediately, to avoid annoying him further. After lunch we climb up a little hill near Herisau and sit over three bottles of beer in a sunny open-air café, which Robert likes, and chat with the proprietress, who rattles on like a sewing machine. To finish, we go to a pastry shop, where he devours eight tartlets with pleasure. Alluding perhaps to his illness, as we say good-bye, he says: "In life there must also be troubles, so that beauty stands out more vividly from the unpleasantness. Worry is the best teacher."

May 16, 1943

ON ROBERT'S SIXTY-FIFTH birthday we agreed that the next time we would take the train through the Ricken Pass to Rapperswil. I already have the tickets in my pocket when at eight in the morning in the Herisau train station I say to him: "So, it's through the Ricken today!" Horrified, he waves me off: "No, no, and what for, anyway? I have been banished to eastern Switzerland and here I'll stay. Why eat trout in Rapperswil when we can have speck in the Appenzellerland?" I give in and say he should choose the route himself. "Let's go to Peterzell, you're sure to like it!" he suggests. "Why not?" and with that we set out with long strides. "How happy I was this morning," Robert says, now entirely cheerful, "when instead of the blue sky I saw clouds! I don't care a fig about superb views and backdrops. When what is distant disappears, what is near tenderly draws nearer. What more do we need to be satisfied than a meadow, a wood, and a few peaceful houses?... And by the way, from now on, come on Sundays, if you can! Now that I no longer practice writing, I cannot afford the extravagance of a weekday walk. It brings disorder into the well-ordered asylum. It really is also quite pleasant to see the world as a Sunday parlor."

To my astonishment, as we walk he begins to talk unprompted about his time in the hospital: "I quite liked being in a sickroom. One lies there like a felled tree. Desires sleep like a child weary from playing. One feels as if in a cloister, or in the antechamber of death. Why should I let them operate on me? I was fine as I was. Except when my fellow patients got something to eat and I got nothing, then I grew a bit waspish. But even that feeling gradually dulled. I am convinced that Hölderlin was not nearly so unhappy in the last thirty years of his life as the literature professors make him out to be. Dreaming the days away in some modest corner, without constant demands, is certainly not martyrdom. People just make it one!"

We hike through Schwellbrun to St. Peterzell, where Robert is delighted by the church, built in 1722, and the elegant priory. We order bratwurst and veal schnitzel, drink a light Tyrolean wine, and order some cake. Over lunch Robert rants for nearly half an hour in response to my remark that a fellow writer was involved in an unhappy love affair during her school days and nearly fell apart as a result: "That baby! Did she have to go and get her heart broken by a complete heel and then trumpet this little *malheur* to the whole world? What an uppity cow! That little literary goose wanted to turn herself into some kind of Swiss poet-Magdalena!"

Under the smoke-gray dome of the sky—fog drifts, not a soul crosses our path—Robert opens up more and more, and he tells me: "My position as a bookkeeper in Wädenswil served as a model for the novel *The Assistant*. From the summer of 1903 to the beginning of January 1904, the work was just about as I described it from memory later in Berlin. I obtained the position through the unemployment office in Zürich, where, after the Wädenswil episode, I worked for a time at the cantonal bank. Max Liebermann told me *The Assistant* was deadly dull. On the other hand he loved *Jakob von Gunten*, for which I gathered my observations while studying at an institute that bears some similarity to the institute portrayed in the novel. The fact that my debut, *Fritz Kocher's Essays*, was sold off cheaply in a West Berlin department store soon after its publication with Insel Verlag was something that my subsequent publisher, Bruno Cassirer, gleefully rubbed in my face. Nonetheless, he published my first poems, with Kari's etchings. Otto von Greyerz then so lambasted my poems in *Bund* that the people sitting with me in the *Blaues Kreuz* turned pale when they told me how I'd been savaged. Those in Zürich? They took no notice of my poems whatsoever. Back then everyone was riding a wave of enthusiasm for Hesse. On his account they let me sink without a trace."

Our conversation also touches on *The Tanners*, of which Robert says: "I wrote it in Berlin in three or four weeks, without revising, so to speak. Some sections that Bruno Cassirer found too boring he threw out, including the episode where Simon finds a clerk's manuscript in the oven. It appeared later in *März*, the magazine that Hermann Hesse formerly coedited. My dear esteemed head doctor Hinrichsen, who saw himself as an important poet, once said to me of that book: 'The first pages are good, but the rest—impossible!' He said this as if he would have choked if he'd had to read the whole thing." Robert laughs heartily at this description. I say how right he was to live like Simon in poverty, simplicity, and freedom, and what a mistake it is when creative people make compromises in favor of their material livelihood. He nods briskly and answers seriously, after a long silence: "Yes, but seen from the outside it's usually a journey from one defeat to another!"

Near Waldstatt, Robert remarks: "Writers without ethics deserve to be whipped. They have sinned against their profession. Now the punishment is that Hitler has been unleashed upon them. Modern literature cannot be spared the accusation that it conducts itself insensitively, arrogantly, and pompously. I am wholly convinced that truly good books could be put in the hands of any reader. Confirmees and old maids, too. But how many products of contemporary *belles lettres* can one say that of?... You see, they're always railing against Marlitt! These are the criticisms of pedants—unfair and narrow-minded. I recently read *In the Counsellor's House* in an old magazine, and I have to say that her liberal mind and her understanding of social changes impressed me. One often finds in such books more tact and feeling than in the award-winning literary doorstoppers. But do you even know Marlitt, who was actually named Eugenie John, and had more adoring fans than simply readers of the weekly magazine *Die Gartenlaube*? It may be that she was a somewhat florid woman and far too convinced of the possibility of progress, but many of today's 'celebrities' have cause to envy her imagination and her progressive spirit. She was supposed to have been a talented singer in the mid-nineteenth century. Then she became gravely ill and wrote nearly all of her books in bed: *Gold Elsie*, *The Old Maid's Secret*, and *The Lady with the Carbuncles*. Would I be wrong to call her the first German feminist, who fought resolutely against class pride and self-satisfied piety? J. V. Widmann also tipped his hat to her in reverence; he loved to tell how once in the Schänzli garden cafe in Bern, a rural wedding party from Emmental toasted Marlitt's health without a trace of irony."

A few remarks from this ramble, which we concluded in two Herisau beer halls: "Polite people usually have something up their sleeves."

"Only through flaws does a person's character take on interesting colors. Wickedness exists to create contrast and thereby to bring life into the world."

"No writer is obliged to perfection. One loves him even with all his human flaws and quirks!" This during a conversation about Jean Paul's *Titan*, whose climbing, vine-like style fascinates Robert.

"Creative types don't bother with theory. This distinguishes them from imitators."

July 27, 1943

ROBERT'S FACE EMACIATED, but brownish-red. His olive-green suit worn out, the trouser cuffs turned up, his shirt collar patched, the inevitable umbrella on his arm; referring to the latter he says by way of welcome: "It wants to go for a walk too—and besides, umbrellas attract good weather!"

We take the train from St. Gallen to Altstätten, chatting of inconsequential things and lighting one cigarette after another. Robert looks up at the receding clouds: "Clouds are my favorite. They're so sociable, like good, silent comrades. At once the sky is livelier—more human."

Lavish breakfast at the St. Margrethen station restaurant, since Robert suggested on the train: "Shall we have a nibble? A morning meal would be just the thing!" We are the only guests. A fat little waitress serves us, almost offended to be disturbed during her breakfast, but greedy for our meal coupons. Robert eats very quickly, spooning up jam right out of the dish. He dips his bread crusts in coffee. We begin our walk on the paved, nearly empty military road. The thirteen kilometers to Alstätten are a stone's throw for us. Robert points out that Appenzell is embraced by the canton of St. Gallen like an island. When he spots a homey tavern, a prosperous farmhouse, or a church with a baroque onion dome, he stops and murmurs: "How beautiful—how charming!" The hilly country and the solemn Sunday quiet seem to make him almost tipsy: "How lovely, when people lay their heavy, clumsy hands in their laps and leave everything to nature!" At nearly every village, contrary to his habit, he asks a lumbering cyclist or a farmer, standing in shirtsleeves in his garden: "What is this village called? This hill?" He asks like a tramp, without stopping long, without even really waiting for the answer. Au, Heerbrugg, and Balgach appear; far up above on a hilly summit the restaurant Meldegg gazes down at us. We reflect for a minute whether we should turn toward Berneck, which looks as if it lies dreaming in an orchard, in order to head for Heiden by way of Reute. But Robert says: "One can't take both the upper and the lower path at the same time! Let us save a few desires for later! It does one good to think of them on workdays!"

Great temptation in Marbach to climb up to the delightfully situated castle Weinstein, enthroned above a vineyard, and to dine there. Robert however suggests that we heroically resist every attraction and continue to Alstätten: "Through this tactic of renunciation we will earn our meal! It is quite stimulating to feel one's stomach sink like an empty balloon." A comely girl passes on a bicycle. Her fluttering skirt exposes her legs. "What a sweet sight, a girl's legs," he smiles to himself. "The purest poem ..." and as I smile back he adds: "Not that I mean anything underhanded by it."

From the church we hear the parish singing, "Holy God, We Praise Thy Name!" Robert remarks: "But it sounds so soulless, like a group of conscripts. If God receives no warmer praise than this, he is to be pitied."

An astounding coincidence: I mention that his brother Karl told me how someone once suggested that Cassirer publish Robert's and Christian Morgenstern's poems with illustrations by Paul Klee. Morgenstern, who at the time was an editor at the Cassirer publishing house, had turned down the suggestion because he found Klee too mannered. Hardly a minute after I had spoken the name "Paul Klee," we pass an empty shopwindow in Balgach, where an advertising board stands with the words: *Paul Klee—carver of wooden candelabra.*

In the Marbach village square are a few garish fairground booths, a carnival game, and temporary market stalls, behind which the salesmen and ladies sit sedately, as if relaxing at home in their living rooms. Wasps swarm around the sweets. I ask a woman: "They must all require coupons?" To which she nods and answers in dialect, almost apologetically, like a mother who has to refuse her child's wish: "All the good stuff, yes—not much longer, God willing!" As we hike on, Robert says: "Was that not the very richness of life, colorful and harmless? Those gay head-scarves, fiery currants, syrup-red candies, those are the things that the people love! The good old ways will never die. Like a fair call from the days of youth, they always return."

In Alstätten we first try the restaurant at the town museum. We're both somewhat limp from the hike. A few bored officers and sergeants sit in the shady garden. No civilians. The proprietress says she can bring us nothing but meatloaf and potato salad. We, however, are hungry for a stout Sunday meal. So onward to Klosterbräu! Two old men sitting over cider; a crucifix on the wall. The innkeeper shuffles by in slippers. He goes to ask in the kitchen if there's anything for us to peck at. Then he calls out: "Someone will be with you soon!" After five minutes we order vermouth, pay, and leave. No one ever came by to let us know about the food. Third try at Frauenhof, a beautiful old building. There we sit in the garden, but the patches of sun dancing on the table make Robert nervous: "Better to scoot over into the shade!" Soup with omelet strips, schnitzel, Brussels sprouts and peas, potatoes, cake and vanilla ice cream. A steaming banquet of the gods, which prompts Robert to remark: "The warm things should be colder and the cold things warmer." We enjoy everything and drink a Neuchâtel wine, whose floral aroma pleases Robert.

Back to Marbach in the blistering heat to see the bustle of the fair again. We go into a restaurant next to a piping carousel, and drink coffee, cider, beer. The voices of the barkers, the squawking of people playing games, the tirades of the "Cheap Jack" merchant tumble down to us willy-nilly in the restaurant. Through the window we see children's close-shorn heads, men's tomato-red pates, girls giggling. As much as he usually seeks out quiet, Robert feels secure amid the loud festival throngs. We take the trolley bus to Heerbrugg, which he finds grandiose. On the streets, young boys mend the broken bicycle tubes of their female companions, prompting Robert to remark: "The troubadours of today!"

The alcohol has washed away the last of his inhibitions. Recalling a pastor from his youth, he says, in dialect: "He was a real swine, always after the women!" He laughs boisterously. In Heerbrugg we order another beer in a dark garden. We come to talk of a schoolteacher who has published sonnets. This circumstance becomes a source of wild hilarity for Robert, as he plucks at my arm and punches the air with amusement: "That little shepherd boy writes sonnets à la Count von Platen! Splendid, how daft people can be. A little schoolmaster wants to give himself classical airs, and turns himself into a laughingstock in front of the whole world. Who does he think he is, Gottfried Keller? How singular was his ability to join the lofty with the common and the democratic, thereby humanizing it! But this teacher and his sonnets …! Have you ever heard of such buffoonery?"

On the ride home we grow quieter with each passing station. Only once, pointing to a wooded hill, Robert whispers: "Are we not returning richer than we left? Was this not a beautiful day?" I stick a little something nice in his pocket. When we say good-bye, I'm suddenly startled by his tragic face. That long handclasp …

A few conversation topics from this Sunday: "My first poems were published just as I wrote them. I was a clerk then, living on the Zürichberg like a monk: reclusive, and often freezing and hungry, too. But I wrote poems later too, particularly in Biel and Bern. Yes, and even in the Waldau asylum I churned out nearly a hundred poems. But the German newspapers wanted nothing to do with them. My clients were at the *Prager Presse* and the *Prager Tageblatt*, Otto Pick and his friend Max Brod. And sometimes Kurt Wolff would print a few verses in his literary yearbook." I tell him he certainly has Franz Kafka to thank for his popularity in Prague as well; Kafka was a fan of Robert's Berlin writings and of *Jakob von Gunten*. But Robert waves this off; he hardly knows Kafka's work.

"In Stuttgart I wrote a pretty little letter to the director of the Hoftheater, asking whether he might grant me a free ticket once in a while. He had me come by, examined me briefly (I hadn't published anything at that point) and summoned the noblesse to grant me a free seat for the whole season." I: "Your beautiful calligraphic handwriting must have been partly to thank for that?" Robert: "Perhaps. It rendered me many an excellent service. Even in school I was famous for it."

"*The Assistant* is an altogether realistic novel. I barely needed to invent anything. Life saw to it for me." He refuses to accept my suggestion that he was in love with the wife of the engineer Tobler: "All thoughts of love and romance were very far from my mind in that novel." He tells of an art dealer A., whom he met in Biel; A. made a great fortune in Berlin and gambled it away quicker than he'd earned it. When Robert was a clerk in Zürich, he sometimes ran into A. and his girlfriend Maria Slavona, the gossamer-fine impressionist painter, who had been a student of Karl Stauffer-Bern. He describes an evening that they spent together on a bench by Lake Zürich; primarily he spent it admiring the voluptuous Slavona's dainty feet.

Briefly he mentions an acquaintanceship with the painter Ernst Morgenthaler, during which he had fallen in love with Morgenthaler's blonde-braided housemaid Hedi. Later, he often wrote her letters. She had been so crisp, so young and naive. The sculptor Hermann Hubacher and his wife were dear old friends from Robert's youth in Biel; many a time he had caught his breath like a steed in the manger of their summer house in Faulensee near Spiez, when on a "trot" from Bern to Thun and onward.

He indulges in a vivid description of a hot air balloon ride that the publisher Paul Cassirer had invited him on before the First World War. They rose up at the fall of dusk from Bitterfeld, well supplied with cold cutlets and beverages, swam peacefully through the night over the slumberous earth and landed the next day on the Baltic coast. He had written a little *feuilleton* about that romantic ride. He was a curious fellow, Paul Cassirer, a mess of hedonism and melancholia; at his parties the Walser brothers were always counted as formidable gluttons.

We speak for a long time of Nestroy. Robert listens with interest as I tell him that in 1855, Nestroy sent a letter to an unknown beauty in Vienna, in which he confessed that he had been so fascinated by the sight of her in a suburban theater that she had become the object of his most ardent desires. Sadly, a "cripple of marriage," he had been sitting next to his wife, so he could not approach her. He had, however, sent his servant after her to find out where she lived and what she was called. Now he was offering himself for a discreet friendship, even if she should happen already to be engaged; a secret friend could be of use even after a honeymoon. Since he found attempting to speak to her directly too common, he suggested the following solution: On a certain day at half past one in the afternoon, both parties would drive in hackney carriages down the main boulevard of the Prater garden in opposite directions, so that they would have to meet underway, presumably in the vicinity of the Rondeau. In order that Nestroy should recognize the beauty's carriage from a distance, she was to let her handkerchief flutter from the right-hand window. This would constitute the sign that she deemed him worthy of a secret liaison. She would recognize him on the boulevard by his light-gray traveling cloak with bright-red lining. On the following day he would use the handkerchief signal to take the next step in the fortification of the desired friendship … After this account, Robert holds forth at length on the gallantry of previous generations. He believes, however, that in this letter Nestroy's urgency had made him look like a buffoon, exposing him as inexperienced in love, indeed indelicate. For "women, if they are not strumpets, wish to be taken dead seriously. And by terming himself a 'cripple of marriage,' Nestroy had shown little tact. The unknown lady must have thought: Such an ungallant husband is someone I hardly want even as a friend!" I: "Do you know about the virulent letters Nestroy hurled at Saphir, the arrogant critic? In one of them he had answered Saphir's barb that in Nestroy's comedy *The Foundling* there had been only four witty thoughts—and they had been Saphir's—with no less venom, saying that if he had needed to steal someone else's jokes, he certainly wouldn't have looked to Saphir: why scrounge them third-hand, when one could get better ones second-hand?" Robert, at this: "Accusations of plagiarism usually come from jealous, impotent types, who wretchedly try to scrape together from others what remains broken in themselves. Why shouldn't a genius help himself to the ideas of others? Often they achieve meaning, form, and life only in the hands of a genius. Nestroy was a master juggler in this game of inspiration. Do you remember the sentence in one of his farces: 'The people are a giant in the cradle, who wakes, stands up, staggers around, stomps on everything, and in the end falls down someplace worse than in the cradle'? There are as many folksy images in his works as carrots in a vegetable garden." I: "Do you know that Nestroy was a fanatical Prussophobe, who used the stage to advance the view that Austria needed to shake off the Prussian yoke?" Robert: "Yes, writers often have uncannily long snouts, which they use to sense the future. They sniff out coming events like pigs sniff out truffles."

October 19, 1943

I USE MY one-day military leave to climb down from the Sargans fort into the valley, where I catch the train to Herisau. Conversation with the head doctor, who tells me that Robert reacted to the news of his brother Karl's death on September 28 in Bern with only a dry "Really!" He has become completely hardened about it, acting the sober realist, since he does not want to stand out from the other asylum residents in any way. He strictly avoids any display of emotion. This behavior is seen, the doctor tells me, in many schizophrenics. Either the emotional balance swings only slightly at joy or sorrow, or the patient has explosive bursts of emotion, sometimes of catastrophic dimension. Robert seems to be deliberately trying to distance himself from his environment. Only news of his sister Lisa's illness seems to have moved him somewhat. At first, the doctor had taken pains to discreetly pass Robert articles that were published about him or about Karl Walser. Eventually Robert had become downright nasty, however, and now ostentatiously refused to greet the doctor. When the doctor tried to talk to him about it—"We got along just fine before, Herr Walser!"—he had flared up: "Why do you pester me with all this wish-wash? Can't you see that I don't care a fig? Leave me in peace! That is all long behind me." Nor did he want to hear anything about his intestinal ulcer. To a question on this subject he had answered irascibly: "Must I be sick? Are you not satisfied to have me in good health? Why do you plague me with such trifles?"

Robert is already waiting impatiently for me in front of the second wing, where his room is. He has not responded to any of my letters or packages in the last six months. But now he walks briskly and easily to meet me, with joyful excitement, in fact: "You smell of the military! Rifle grease, leather, straw, sweat—it reminds me of home. It's beautiful, isn't it, to live so intimately with the people, body to body, like brothers?" He inquires with interest about everything on my person: from the rolled tent-cloth and flashlight swinging from my belt to the new peaked cap and insignia. I tell him I have always been attracted to the simple life of the military. Robert: "That is truly one of its most positive aspects. Abundance can be so oppressive. True beauty, the beauty of the everyday, reveals itself most delicately in poverty and simplicity." In the afternoon, over a farewell drink at the St. Gallen train station, he speaks of aging: "Remarkably few people understand how to enjoy aging, though it can be such a joy. In age one understands that the world always seeks to return to the simple, elementary things. A healthy instinct struggles against the domination of the exceptional or the strange. The restless lust for the opposite sex has burned out, leaving only the desire for the comforts of nature and the beautiful, concrete things that are within reach of anyone who longs for them. Finally vanity has disappeared, and one sits in the great tranquility of age as in the mild light of a mock sun."

In the morning: as we make our way at a quick pace through the old part of Herisau, past the barracks toward St. Gallen, we speak first of the horrors of the current war, then of the Swiss people. I say: "In reality, the masses don't want to rule at all. They want to be ruled." Robert enthusiastically agrees: "In fact they are quite generously disposed toward tyranny." But immediately he adds: "But one may not say that. Or else the masses take one for a consummate boor and grow nasty. At heart, they desire far less freedom than they pretend." He defends the bourgeoisie's right to exist. Philistines are the guardians of a civilization that has taken refuge with them. Nothing of great or lasting value has come of gypsying around. Since in their small town parochialism, bourgeois people show no interest in the literary testaments of the big city, the modern literati have taken revenge by making fun of them and turning them into the objects of their poison-filled pens. Such writers lack the good-natured, conciliatory, serene humor of a Carl Spitzweg, a Wilhelm Raabe, a Martin Usteri, or a Gottfried Keller. These big-city ranters have become unbearably arrogant, noisy, and high-handed. And that is precisely what art must never become. It must adapt to the universal order and be a guardian of that order, just as the bourgeoisie is, unconsciously. As enervating as this stultification can sometimes be, Philistines have long been more tolerable than the literary types who believe it's their duty to teach the world.

In Haggen, a rural suburb of St. Gallen, which we reach by the old and new bridges over the Sitter—Robert is excited to show me the beautiful calligraphic inscriptions from the eighteenth century and the colorful magic of the autumn woods—he suggests taking our morning pint at the Schlössli. We admire the house, which dates from the seventeenth century, and its chests, coats of arms, religious paintings, and old engravings. A girl from Ticino brings us strong apple cider. We chat a bit with her. When I ask her whether she is homesick, Robert answers in her place: "Homesick? No. Homesickness is a stupid thing!"

We reach St. Gallen around midday through fog. The fresh air and the lush fruit trees lining the path have a stimulating effect on Robert. During the meal at Weinfalken, which we wash down with a crisp Maienfelder wine, we talk of Jeremias Gotthelf, whom Robert once again violently attacks. He says he usually cannot read him with pleasure. Robert is increasingly offended by Gotthelf's tendency to pour his pastoral sauce over everything. He couldn't stand to see anyone rise beside him; he tried to push everyone else into the grave. Gottfried Keller and C. F. Meyer were like him in that way. What could be more thought-provoking than *Green Henry*, which he finds "appallingly beautiful"! More beautiful with each passing year. Then he praises J. V. Widmann's urbane noblesse. Compared to him, many of today's *feuilleton* editors are characterless, ambitious speculators—without loyalty and without a love of solid poetic craftsmanship. How often have people rubbed Robert's nose in his lack of success! Whenever he was invited to dine, or dragged to a salon, people gave him advice, whether loudly or softly, acting the good citizen or full of patronizing self-importance, to write in this or that style in order to finally make a career for himself! In such circles originality has no great market value. From Goethe to Eichendorff and Rudolf Herzog, various poets have been touted as good models for him, by Max Slevogt too, who mocked Robert's poorly received books with Bavarian solidity. Even his publisher, Bruno Cassirer, suggested he take Gottfried Keller's novella technique as an example. Yes, lack of success is a furious, dangerous snake—pitilessly, it tries to strangle whatever is true and original in an artist. Once, the publishers of the magazine *Die Woche* invited him to submit a novel. He was asked to send with it a request for an honorarium. In response he sent *The Assistant*, and named eight thousand marcs as his price. Two days later the manuscript was returned without a note. At this, he stormed into the publisher's office to inquire as to the meaning of this mute *retourpost*. When the publisher began, with the loftiness of an officer, to make fun of the requested honorarium, Robert grew brazen: "You camel! You understand nothing whatsoever of literature!" and, slamming the door, he left the room without a good-bye. Shortly thereafter Cassirer published the novel.

Robert tells me that he borrowed the two-hundred-year-old nautical novel *The Adventures of Roderick Random* from the asylum library. Its author, Tobias Smollett, a Scottish ship's doctor who married a hot-blooded creole woman, was strongly influenced by Lesage and Cervantes, having translated *Gil Blas* and *Don Quixote*, but his gift for trenchant storytelling, which often slips into brilliant caricature, makes for very entertaining reading. In general, Robert says, he has often been stimulated as much by mediocre books as by first-rate ones. Perhaps it is similar for the reading public. Instinctively, they dismiss genius: "That is why second- or third-rate talents usually achieve success faster than the first-rate ones. Everything about the character of a genius is uncomfortable; and the people love comfortability."

Conversation about Karl Walser. Robert urges me to tell him about my last visit to his brother. "It was at the end of July in his studio in Zürich on Stampfenbachstrasse," I say. "We sat on the terrace, with a view of the Limmat and of Platzspitz park. Karl maintained that he could only paint frescos in the city. In the country he would go fishing, take walks, laze about—but certainly not paint. The two years he spent in Twann inspired nothing more than a few paintings. He was disturbed also by all the greenery, as he never painted directly from nature. Pointing to his forehead, he added: 'One must have nature in here, like poetry. Yes, the impressionists, they could sit right in front of the meadows, flowers, and trees; for them, the elves and pucks were still very much alive. But in our time? A city dweller can no longer allow himself to simply sit around in nature. He must make nature himself.' Painting frescoes was devilishly hard work, he said. Moreover, he had been given too much Cibazol for a bout of pneumonia. This had ruined his heart, so that now he could no longer smoke or drink alcohol. He had degenerated, through gritted teeth, into a goody-goody, and really wasn't supposed to paint frescoes anymore anyway. For it would mean his death. But he would rather kick the bucket than fail to do the work he had promised for the Bern Stadttheater. When I told him that I liked the busts that Hermann Haller and Hermann Hubacher made of him, he answered: 'Really? That surprises me. Haller in particular struggled with his. A good dozen sittings, during which I bridled at being measured like a breeding bull. Anyway, I'm not the sculptural type, but rather pictorial, difficult to grasp.' Once in Berlin he had received an offer to become a lecturer in theater painting at an art school in Hamburg. He had answered: 'In the provinces? Out of the question!' Max Pechstein too had declined the call. Nowadays he regretted this negative attitude, as after ten years of work he would have gotten a proper pension, which he could well use." Robert asks how his brother had responded to Hitler. "Like the book designer E. R. Weiss, no doubt. Karl recounted how Weiss growled: 'Oh really—he can kiss my ass!' He was arrested shortly thereafter. He was however soon released. But do you know," I ask Robert, "how your brother fared in Vienna? When he returned to Switzerland from Berlin, he lived for a while on St. Peter's Island in Lake Biel, which you so love. Then he received an offer to paint the house of the millionaire C. in Vienna. 'Lovely,' your brother said, 'My wife and I left right away. C. lived in a gilded palace. I was led into a huge ceremonial hall. A little man burst in, embraced me, and cried: "Ah, *Meister*! How good that you have come!" This was C., profiteering personified. His mistress at that time was a well-known novelist, whose bedroom contained a diamond-studded golden Buddha. Appalling. At the same time, dozens of people were starving to death in Vienna every day. Eventually, the novelist could no longer stand living in that swank house, and silently ran away. To replace her, C. picked up a fifteen-year-old off the street, who betrayed him every chance she got. His jealousy led to his death, shortly thereafter, of a stroke ... But my wife and I nearly starved to death in his gold palace. Precious silver platters, but nothing on them. When I complained of this to C., he told me he had sent me the best apples, pies, and poultry, but the cook had given it all away to a fat priest. She was the one I should be giving a good thrashing.'"

We buy ripe garden pears for Robert in the marketplace, continue to the Pfund pastry shop, and finally settle down for a farewell drink in the station restaurant. There Robert says: "You don't take my sorties against Jeremias Gotthelf amiss, do you? He remains a great phenomenon in spite of everything I say. But his constant grumbling and disdainfulness goes against my whole being. I simply like the world as it is, with all its virtues and vices."

January 2, 1944

"SHALL WE PAY our respects to Hölderlin today?" I ask. Robert replies: "Hölderlin? What a delightful idea! Hopefully we won't get as soaked as I did last Sunday afternoon, when a veritable deluge poured down on me. I returned to the asylum like the lousiest tramp." Today, too, despite the cold, he has brought neither overcoat nor umbrella. He looks rather raffish in his worn-out yellow-checked suit, gentian blue shirt, red-striped tie, and rolled-up trousers.

We strike out briskly on the lightly snow-covered street that leads to Gossau; a white weasel shoots past, burrows a bit in the snow, and peeks curiously up at us, ears perked. We speak first of the bombing of German cities. I remark that I find it disgraceful to wage war in the interior of a country, against women, children, and sick people, regardless of what nation is doing it. The fact that Hitler's people bombed London does not entitle the Allies to employ the same inhumane tactics. Robert counters fiercely, saying that I judge the situation subjectively, and too sentimentally. Anyone who is threatened the way the British are must turn to the most ruthless realpolitik. Hitler's Huns deserve no better. Every nation, in merely deciding to exist, becomes brutally egotistical; in this even Christianity has to take a back seat. I: "Did the civilized peoples fight back when the Italians went at the Abyssinians with bomber squadrons?" Robert: "Allow me the observation that the Abyssinians wouldn't have fallen into that position had they resisted the temptations of civilization and had remained loyal to tradition. It's a matter of loyalty to tradition, always and everywhere!"

With pleasure Robert shows me the beautiful old part of the village of Gossau. Most of the people are in church. It is very quiet: only a few sledding children and interned Poles in their yellow-green uniforms. We hike onward, now and then meeting a farmer's sleigh, the horse's harness jingling; the snow often comes to our knees. A farmhand shouldering a dung fork comes out of a stable. I call out: "Mornin'!" He doesn't answer, which prompts Robert to remark: "He's probably jealous that he's not out for a stroll like us!" In Arnegg we knock at the door of a tavern. But it remains deathly silent. Two hours later we are in Hauptwil, where Hölderlin was tutor to the Gonzenbach family around 1800. There is a baroque-style bourgeois house with a sundial containing the motto:

> Work and wake, long as it's light,
> For I don't tell the hours of the night.

Across from it lies the Zum Leuen inn. We get excellent coffee and sharp Tilsit cheese. Robert asks me: "Don't you think the proprietress comes from southern Germany? I suspect it from her dialect. Perhaps Hölderlin brought Württembergians here with him." We stop in front of the ample patrician house of the Gonzenbach family, who settled here at the beginning of the seventeenth century and grew rich in the canvas business, admiring the little tower through which the street passes, and the Venetian balconies, the quiet courtyard, the peaceful facade of the stately home with its double staircase and weathervane. The estate is now occupied by a school of home economics run by a charitable society, but Robert finds that the house has kept its painting-like quality, its grand and dreamy feel. I: "Shall we look at the Hölderlin plaque they put up last year?" Robert waves off this idea: "No, no, let us not bother with such placard nonsense! How repugnant are things that make a show of reverence. And by the way, Hölderlin's was only one of many human fates to play out here. A famous person must not cause one to forget the unfamous."

We stand gawking for a good quarter of an hour, and as we turn on a side street toward the wooded hill that separates Hauptwil from Bischofszell, we ask an elderly man who is shoveling snow in front of his house whether there are any remaining descendants of the estate's former owners. He looks at us through his right eye—the left is blind—and answers: "Yes, there's one. But he's nearly deaf and has gone a bit soft," and after a bit he adds, "People don't deserve such a splendid house, now, when they're dropping bombs on everything." I say: "Perhaps they'll improve, gradually ..." The man: "Them, improve?" I: "Perhaps they'll be forced to improve!" He: "Indeed. That could be. We can only hope!" and Robert nods.

It's now close to noon. During the hike I finally tell Robert (it has been on the tip of my tongue for a while but I wanted to wait for a psychologically opportune moment, so as not to upset him) that his sister Lisa, who lies fatally ill in a Bern hospital, had expressed the wish that he and I might come and visit her one last time. He refuses immediately: "Eh, more of this to-do! I neither may nor wish to travel to Bern again, after being thrown out, so to speak. It's a point of honor. I have been staked down in Herisau and I have my daily duties here, which I do not wish to neglect. Only not to attract attention, not to disturb the order of the asylum! That I cannot allow myself ... Anyway: sentimental requests leave me cold. Am I not also sick? Do I not also need my rest? In such cases it is best to remain all on one's own. Nor did I want it otherwise when I was admitted to the hospital. In such situations simple people like us must behave as quietly as possible. And now I'm supposed to 'trot off' with you to Bern, of all things? I would embarrass myself in front of you! We'd stand there like two idiots with poor Lisa, maybe we'd even make her cry. No, no, as fond as I am of her, we mustn't give in to such feminine fripperies! It is enough for us simply to take walks together, don't you think?" I: "But things are bad with Lisa, very bad. Perhaps you'll never see her again …!" Robert: "Well then by God, we'll never see each other again. Such is human fate. I too will have to die alone one day. I'm sorry about Lisa, of course. She was a wonderful sister to me. But her sense of family borders on the pathological, the immature." Later: "We Walsers are all so excessively fragile and hung up on family ties. Haven't you ever noticed: childless couples—and we Walsers are all childless—usually remain somewhat childlike themselves. A person (at least a healthy one) grows up when he cares about other people. Cares give his life depth. Childlessness in our family is a typical symptom of overrefinement, which is also expressed, among other ways, in maximum sensitivity." We eat at a butcher shop in Bischoffszell, after taking in the grandiose town hall. A miniature Christmas tree still stands in the dining room. There is meat soup, veal in mushroom cream sauce, peas, a kind of *pommes frites*, salad, and fruit compote. Accompanying it, the spirited red Nussbaumer wine of the region. We are served by the proprietor's very pregnant wife. Robert tells me that a sergeant from the unit he served in, now a bookkeeper in Basel, had sent him cheroots for Christmas. How could he have known the address? They had heard nothing from each other for decades. But the little package had awakened many memories. And then on New Year's Day a farmer from Glarus in his ward had sung old folk songs, including a romantic courtly ballad from the middle ages. Robert had however withdrawn as much as possible from the actual communal Christmas festivities, and from the church service; it was too much activity for him.

* * *

Train ride from Bischofszell to Gossau, where we feast on sweets in a pastry shop. I tell Robert about reading Erich Eyck's three-volume work on Bismarck, which contains the remark, concerning the year 1852: Bismarck wanted to destroy the big cities with their revolutionary inhabitants wholesale. I tell him that I am increasingly of the opinion that Bismarck was a forerunner of Hitler's people: a cynical pettifogger and, when it suited him, a brutal power politician and warmonger. Admittedly, Bismarck was a hundred times more clever and cultivated than the Nazis. Robert agrees and says that Mussolini strikes him as an Italian version of Count Bismarck. National socialism really began with Frederick the Great.

Robert asks me if I would mind if we take a path through the meadows from Gossau to Herisau to cool our wine-fogged heads. I agree. We trudge through deep snow toward a wooded area on a hill; between sturdy blackish trees we stumble upon the stone that marks the border between the Cantons of Appenzell Outer Rhodes and St. Gallen. Robert brushes it tenderly and asks twice: "Was this not a nice day?" In Herisau we still have an hour and a half until my train leaves. We dither about whether to go to the station restaurant. I suggest we go up to the village instead. Robert agrees gladly. We decide on the pub Drei Könige in the old part of town. There is only one waitress, who sits writing a letter. It's cozy: warm and dim. Robert feels well taken care of, and his face looks refreshed and alive. He drinks three "large darks," one after another, and smokes the sergeant's cheroots. He talks for almost an hour of Bern: "Yes, I lived there for nearly eight years, until I was hauled off to Waldau, where I stayed three and a half years and even wrote a bit at first—not much, just enough to continue to serve my clientele: in the Bern years that included above all the *Berliner Tageblatt*, which paid princely sums, and the *Prager Tageblatt*, which paid poorly. But they took everything of mine, and that trust was worth more to me than the better honoraria I got from the Swiss newspapers, whose editors often grumbled about my pieces. In Biel I wrote mainly for various magazines. You see, every time I went to a new city, I forgot my past and adapted completely to the new milieu. In Bern I had to fight hard, for years. At my age it's no small thing to forge a new home for oneself. I came to Bern as poor as a church mouse, since the few thousand marcs I had put away in a bank went straight down the drain thanks to inflation. Yes, I lived quite alone, and changed lodgings often. Surely over a dozen times. Sometimes the places were truly shabby. My most frequent companions were waitresses and the daughter of a Jewish publisher, as well as the librarian Hans Bloesch and sometimes the writer A. F., who was completely shameless. I should have socked him. I made a tremendous effort to get back on my feet and hunt down pretty bits of inspiration. But I also let a lot of alcohol flow down my gullet, which meant that here and there I soon found myself unwelcome." I: "Oh, did you go on some real benders?" Robert: "Certainly! The majority of what I took in as honoraria I washed down again in alcohol. What one won't do when lonely! Over the weekends or at holidays I would sometimes go to my sister's in Bellelay; but other than that I rarely saw my family."

I ask Robert whether it is true that in Berlin he burned the unpublished manuscripts of three novels. "That is quite possible. In those days I was hell-bent on writing novels. But I came to understand that my heart was set on a form that was too expansive for my talents. So I withdrew into the snail shell of short stories and *feuilletons* ... By the way: It is up to the author alone to decide which literary genre he should turn himself to. Perhaps he writes such novels only so that he can finally have enough air to breathe. It is quite irrelevant whether the rest of the world says yes or no. If one wins, one must also be able to lose ... If I could start over, I would do my best to eliminate subjectivity, and write for the good of the people. I gave myself too much liberty. One must not try to sidestep the people. The terrible beauty of *Green Henry* stands before me as an example."

"In Herisau," Robert adds, "I stopped writing. What for? My world was shattered by the Nazis. The newspapers I wrote for are gone; their editors have been chased away or are dead. And so I've become practically a fossil."

Three remarks: "Human reason awakens only in poverty."

"Writers of genius foretell world history like prophets."

"Dependence has something good-natured about it; independence inspires enmity."

On the way to the train station I tell him that on New Year's Day I saw a French farce in Zürich. The infidelity motif of Parisian boulevard authors, now long pat, came off as rather clunky in German, however. Robert: "I'm sick to death of this motif. But perhaps the infidelity is there to keep the women awake. Otherwise they would get sleepy." During the conversation we pass a child pulling a sled, who looks at us with big eyes. Robert asks me: "Did you see his eyes? It's as if he guessed our mischievous mood!"

As we part he says: "Until next time—if we survive that long!" I: "Are you in doubt? We may both live to be ancient." Robert: "Hopefully ... and we'll still have many beautiful times together. Beauty usually offers itself to those who seek it."

May 25, 1944

ON JANUARY 7, Robert's sister Lisa died in Bern. From what I know of him, he would rather tear out his tongue than speak of her death. But how dear she was to him is written in *The Tanners*, where the character of Hedwig the teacher is an intimate depiction of this self-sacrificing, matronly, altruistic woman.

With some difficulty I wangle a day and a half of leave to visit Robert. My unit is currently stationed in Seewis. I join in the morning march up the 2400-meter Vilan. Radiant spring sky. An enchanting carpet of gentian, daffodils, cyclamen, and campion in the midst of the froth of fruit-tree blossoms in the valley of Seewis. As I return to the village, weighed down by my machine gun, the square in front of the patrician town hall, where we are quartered, is filled with bleating sheep, goats, and phlegmatic cows. In the middle, a young veterinarian with a syringe. I throw on my Sunday uniform and dash to the Valzeina train station. On the train I doze listlessly. I arrive in Herisau in the evening. The new head doctor, Dr. Heinrich Künzler, is out today, so I cannot speak to him until tomorrow. I lodge at the guesthouse Zum Hörnli, which also runs a butcher shop. The bald proprietor sits in a butcher's bib and shirtsleeves, cards in hand, playing *Jass*. I ask, "Can I stay here?" and he looks me over from head to foot like an ox before answering: "Yes!" The plumpness of both his wife and the waitress inspires some hope of culinary pleasures. On my evening walk I pass the armory. Between high stacks of wood, thirty or so boys are drumming, most of them barefoot. They're practicing for the children's festival with earnest diligence. A patient instructor attempts to teach some of the clumsier ones the most primitive drumroll. A few half-wits listen, including a boy with the face of a fifty-year-old. Grinning, he circles the drummers on a scooter. A small, gray-haired cretin taps his forehead with a wink, as if to say the drummer boys aren't right in the head. A few old men salute from the almshouse when I pass in uniform. Excellent evening meal at Hörnli. The proprietor says he would rather close shop than serve his guests the paltry seventy grams of meat mandated by the officials. As I lie down to sleep I hear the *Jass* players thundering on the table; it sounds as if the house is about to jump off its foundations.

Early in the morning a conversation with the head doctor, who believes Robert's ulcer has shrunk rather than grown. Appetite and weight remain consistent. A walk to St. Gallen via Winkeln and Bruggen. Muggy, dismal gray weather. Robert unshaven, with gray stubble on his sullen face. A silent struggle to overcome his suspicion because of my conference with the doctor. He speaks voluntarily only when I tell him that a collection of money has been taken up for the playwright Georg Kaiser. He is of the opinion that generally only large sums should be accepted: "Small sums provoke ridicule and lead to debasement. Personally I would rather live in squalor than have to say '*Merci!*' to paltry donations. Earning money oneself is better than taking it from others." Humorously he mimes someone haughtily taking a coin from the pocket of his waistcoat, only to give the gift a contemptuous kick with his foot. I ask Robert about the Fountain of Justice in Biel, which had recently come up in a conversation with one of my comrades in arms, the sculptor Franz Fischer. "It stands in front of the gothic town hall and dates from the beginning of the eighteenth century. Really an outstanding piece of work. In those days the spirit of genius still lived among the people, and an artist was content to be a solid, anonymous craftsman. The artists of today don't know how much they've lost along with their modesty." Next, a conversation about Schiller's "Song of the Bell," which Robert recently reread. He admires Schiller's skill as a prophet and his folksy expressive power. He has a bit of both in him: Franz Moor and Karl Moor, Tell and Gessler. The ability to express complicated things lightly and clearly is doubtless a sign of genius.

Räss cheese and cider in the Rössli in Bruggen; an aperitif in a St. Georgen pub. As we continue walking, Robert enthuses about the romantic gorge, as well as the woodland paths and meadow tracks. In St. Gallen he stops for a long time in front of the house where the reformer Vadian lived and died, and whispers: "Charming—charming! Above all: How lovely are cities when the people are all at home around their noontime tables! The quiet of the streets has something so sweet and mysterious about it. What other adventure does one need!"

Elegant lunch at the station restaurant with Châteauneuf du Pape. Robert tells me that in the Waldau asylum he'd once earned spontaneous applause from the women for sawing wood. After the death of Professor Wilhelm von Speyr, with whom he'd gotten along well, differences soon arose between himself and the new director, Professor Jakob Klaesi, with the result that in the summer of 1933 he was transported to Herisau under escort. He speaks at length of Heinrich Zschokke's *Look at the Self*, in which Zschokke mocks Heinrich von Kleist's reading of the play *Schroffenstein* in Bern. Moving on to the Russians: "The idea that those who are supposedly strong and triumphant are in reality weak, yet paradoxically hold the reins of power, appears throughout czarist literature. For example in Tolstoy's *Anna Karenina* or Dostoevsky's *The Eternal Husband*." Of the aerial bombardments of Berlin he remarks: "Perhaps these barbarities have the advantage of leading the residents of the big cities back to a more intuitive, more natural life. How much of the musty past has been dragged along through the centuries! Besides, it can't do the Germans any harm to come under a foreign yoke once more. Even cultivated nations have to learn to obey, in order to be able to rule later."

A stop for beer in the forest-dark garden restaurant Zur Harfe, where I remark to Robert: "What an arrogant waitress!" He responds: "I think reserve is absolutely advisable in this case. One often gets much further with it than with pushiness." I then tell him the following story: In Sevelen, where I was stationed, lives an Amazon, who runs a farm with her sister: she's a flat-chested, energetic woman who sticks out from the other villagers in every way, including in her dress. She always wears trousers and a kind of Tyrolean hat with a chinstrap. Apparently she once worked at a Hungarian estate. She returned home with a burning passion for horses—stallions, in particular. One day, as she rode across the fields on her stallion, it tried to mount a mare that was trotting proudly past, hitched to a vehicle. In a single movement the woman threw herself from the coach box onto the stallion's back and masterfully separately the animals. Apparently many people from the area come to the two sisters for faith healing. The authorities don't dare to interfere.

July 24, 1944

A WALK TO Lake Constance. Robert arrives in a tizzy at the place we've agreed to meet and apologizes many times for his lateness. He had only been informed of my telephone call this morning: "Probably some bit of subordinate deviltry! People who feel frustrated by their low status and can't see their dreams realized look for any opportunity to wrong-foot those under them. Their schadenfreude satisfies their personal cravings for revenge."

It is a morose, rain-gray day, which makes the green of the fruit trees seem even more luscious. We have difficulty keeping our way in the jumble of paths. We alternate between woodland trails, meadow tracks, and gullies. Our shoes grow dirtier and dirtier. Nonetheless, we are both very cheery, and chat excitedly in the pugnacious wind.

Robert makes fun of some new publishers that make themselves out to be the boy scouts of literature, "with short pants and jaunty ties. For someone like Schiller, who stormed onto the scene, they can barely manage a smile." He grows excited talking of the "droll mastery" of writers like Charles Dickens or Gottfried Keller, with whom one is never quite sure whether to laugh or cry. This is clearly a sign of genius. I add: "One often doesn't know with your books either." He stops on the road with a fierce jolt and beseeches me with dead earnesty: "No, no! I must implore you not to say my name in connection with such masters. Don't even whisper it. It makes me want to crawl into a hole, being named in such company." Referring to Paul Morand, the author of novellas and travel pieces who was just appointed French Ambassador in Bern, he says: "Presumably one could never raise a Swiss author to such a post. We lack a sense of proportion and tradition. We wallow in our feelings of inferiority. We're either abrasive and cheeky or too modest. Neither is what democracy calls for." Furthermore, he is of the opinion that a society life is poison to an artist. It leads to degeneration and compromise. He sees Nietzsche as a diabolical person, addicted to victory and boundlessly ambitious: "He definitely possessed that seductive quality characteristic of genius. But from the very beginning he cozied up to the devil, which is to say the losers in society, for he felt himself a loser. He was not a man of sunlight. Aggrieved at his lowly status, he became cocky and perverse. For women, his master morality is certainly the most offensive thing imaginable: the perfidious revenge of the unloved." Basel helped shape Nietzsche. "By the way, when at eighteen I was a bankboy in Basel, my brother Oscar once invited me to visit him in Lucerne. Do you know what blazes brightest in my memory from that trip? The sunshine yellow of the crème that we were served for dessert at his boarding house. Does that not remind one of Van Gogh?" As we reach the church in Arbon, an air-raid siren wails. We hear the crack of antiaircraft guns on the far shore of Lake Constance. Robert grows quiet. We duck into a pastry shop to test the cheese- and rhubarb cakes. Later, fish at a lakeside restaurant. In the adjacent hall, American airmen are being fed: robust, broad-shouldered youths. We go for a swim in the baths, where we're the only patrons. Robert climbs up the high dive with his skinny legs, but then climbs back down, remarking: "Let's not be too daring! I have to give up such jumps now. I used to swim often in secluded bays, by night and by day, particularly in Wädenswil and Biel. But now I swim rarely. One can overdo even hygiene."

Return by train to St. Gallen via Rorschach, where we enjoy ourselves in several bars until evening.

December 28, 1944

A BITINGLY COLD, cloudless winter morning. In the hallway we debate where to go. Robert is coatless, with blue-red hands and cheeks and white stubble on his chin. He asks, half-smiling, half-suspiciously, whether I have a set plan: "Did you have any particular idea?" I: "No, nothing!" Robert: "What about Appenzell?... But that's too far for today! Should we climb up or go to St. Gallen?" I: "Do you feel like the city today?" Robert: "Actually, I do!" I: "Off we go, then!" Robert, after a few steps: "Let us take a bit more moderate tempo! We're not trying to chase down beauty. It should accompany us like a mother with a child." I: "But you should have dressed more warmly, Herr Walser!" Robert: "I'm padded with warm underthings. I've always had a horror of overcoats. By the way, I once had a coat like the one you're wearing—back in Berlin, when I slipped briefly into the gentleman's life. Later, in Biel, when I lived in the same room in the Blaues Kreuz that I had lived in before, I practically never lit a fire, not even in the bitterest cold. I put on my army coat and worked no better and no worse than other people do by a stove. On my feet I wore a kind of slippers that I made myself from scraps of clothing. Modern man has, in my opinion, become far too sophisticated. War has at least this in its favor—it forces people back to simplicity. Would we be able to chat undisturbed on the road, free from the stink of gasoline and the cursing of motorists, if gasoline wasn't rationed? There is far too much traveling nowadays in the first place. Hordes of people barge shamelessly into foreign landscapes as if they were the legitimate occupants."

We strike out toward Abtwil. The frost-covered garden hedges hang like airy fishing nets in a landscape delicate as a watercolor. The trees look ready to float into the sky like balloons at any moment. Occasionally we pass a farmer or a peasant woman, implausibly small, almost gnomelike in the silence. Sometimes for a minute or two the fog wraps us in its shroud. Then we see the sun hovering in the south again like a dematerialized ball. An avenue of poplars. On a rowanberry tree some cherry-red berries still hang like corals. From atop a round hill the windows of a few farms flash through the fluttering fog: silver eyes, which gaze magically at Robert. Several times he asks: "Should we go up there?" I: "Why not? Whatever pleases you, pleases me too." Robert: "No, let us stay in the valley! We'll save this delightful adventure for later! Is it not also pleasurable to gaze up at beauty from below? In youth one is hungry for excitement. One confronts the everyday almost like an enemy. With age, on the other hand, one trusts the everyday more than the holiday. The usual is dear, and the unusual makes one suspicious. Thus people change, and it's a good thing that they change."

We pass waterfalls that have turned to ice as if by magic. As we climb through a wood, Robert is suddenly overcome by the desire to leave the path and roam crisscross through brush and past ochre screes, across little brooks and over fallen trees down to the Sitter. He now seems as venturesome and carefree as a boy; he often stops, murmuring: "How homey—how magical!"

Over the Wienerberg and down to St. Gallen, where we wind up at Hotel Schiff for lunch. Over red Berneck wine Robert tells me of the democratic politician Robert Blum—a gentle man, a theatre usher in Leipzig—who was court martialled and shot in 1848. In contrast to him, Bismarck was Kaiser Wilhelm I's loyal sheepdog. Robert believes that the Allies will have a bitterly hard time defeating the Germans on their own soil: "Defending swells the chest. Anyone who fights for his motherland draws from her secret powers. How much nobler is the defense than the offense! Invaders constantly affront and injure, get befuddled, and have to goad themselves on by unnatural means!" He thinks little of his countrymen as they are today. He says, word for word: "A mass of snot-nosed brats and rogues. Without a good master they are good for nothing."

In the asylum library he recently read two books with great interest: the novel *The Ironmaster* by Georges Ohnet, which really was a bit sentimental and kitschy, but the tale was woven admirably. It reminded him of the painter Gustave Courbet. The second book was *Uncle Tom's Cabin*, by Harriet Beecher Stowe, which he calls brilliantly naive. It helped set off the American Civil War.

Over café crème at the Pfund pastry shop, he makes fun of our literary clubs and students who wanted to invite a notorious Nazi writer to read. It is quite right, he thinks, that the authorities forbade his entry: "Anyway, how ridiculous to let a derivative foreign writer parade himself here! And he's not even representative of Germany. Our editors and the 'polite' society have once again allowed a high-caliber tinsel-talent from the Third Reich to put one over on them. You find, by the way, the same lack of imagination and failure of discovery in the literary foundations. It's always the same bunch of goats crowding the manger." Back to Herisau on foot. The sun now glints warm on the little meadow paths that lead us toward Winkeln. As we walk, Robert tells me how his brother Karl was sent by the Cassirer publishing house to Japan with the writer Bernhard Kellerman to illustrate the latter's travelogues. In the middle of a public square in Moscow, Karl gave comrade Kellerman a ringing slap in the face because he had grown arrogant. A bit later the publisher Samuel Fischer had sent for Robert and asked: "Would you like to go to Poland and write a book about it?" Robert: "What for? I like it just as well in Berlin!" I: "Or would you like to travel to Turkey?" Robert: "No, *merci*! One can act like a Turk in other places too, perhaps even more so than in Turkey. I wish to go absolutely nowhere. Why should writers travel, as long as they have imagination?" I add, casually: "I have often come across this attitude in your books, by the way, for example where you say: 'Does nature go abroad? I'm always looking at the trees and telling myself: They aren't leaving either, so why shouldn't I be permitted to remain?'*" Robert: "Yes, only the journey to oneself is important."

Then he talks for a long time of a kind woman, now old, who was friends with his sister Lisa and who has occasionally visited him in the asylum. Her son became an honest, useful man, a mechanic, and the woman now lives with him in Basel. "How

* From *The Tanners*, trans. Susan Bernofsky (two quotes combined).

often in youth does one underestimate such quiet, inconspicuous characters! And yet they are the ones that keep humanity together—they are the source of the strength that keeps a nation fit for life."

April 9, 1945

A FINE BLUE early spring day, as imagined by Mörike:

> I see the clouds changing and the river
> The sun's golden kiss pierces
> Deep into my veins;
> My eyes, wonderfully drunk,
> Sink as if falling asleep;
> Only my ear keeps listening to sound of the bees.

Robert is waiting for me in a new Marengo suit that his sister Fanny gave him for Christmas. His hair is cut short. I say how young he looks today. He smiles, pleased, but speaks little on the way to St. Fiden. We turn right onto the street to Speicherschwendi. It is comfortingly lonesome. A farmer, herding a few goats into the city; a schoolboy shoveling horse manure for his two-wheeled cart; a peddler woman with stringy gray hair lugging a little notions shop on her round back. The reflection of light on a bubbling silver woodland brook, the scattered homesteads in the curved landscape, and the view of Lake Constance in the dull gray distance make Robert almost reverent: "This is the strangest time, early spring, when everything is full of promise and full of tender hope! How easy it is to hike now! It's no longer cold, but not yet warm, the birds awaken and sing, clouds roam with us, and people's faces finally look a little brighter."

We have a morning snack in Rehetobel. I ask a man in the pub about Egon Z. ... He says he's been locked up in the Thurgau insane asylum for several years now. His father was far too strict with him. Egon was sent to first grade at five years old; later the long walk to Trogen for school every day—it took an enormous toll on his nerves. Robert listens with interest. Afterward we climb down into the wooded gorge, on whose far side Trogen lies. Far above us, a dogfight. The farmers stop their work and stare at the sky. Robert, on the other hand, turns to the fir trees and flowers, the clean little Appenzell houses and the steep rocky slopes. For him the whole morning walk is one great delight.

Lunch at Schäfli in Trogen. We both have a huge appetite and clean every plate: the oatmeal soup, the bratwursts, the mashed potatoes, the beans, and the pear compote. At the neighboring table a few soldiers are talking of the collapse of Nazi power. Robert remarks to me: "At some point this silly Hitler-worship had to come home to roost. Anyone exalted to the skies the way he was must eventually fall into the abyss. Hitler hypnotized himself into a cynical complacency, which left no room whatsoever for the well-being of the people." Then he thinks of Raimund's *The Spendthrift*, which he once saw in Berlin with sets by his brother Karl. Girardi played the master carpenter Valentin, who takes in the poverty-stricken count whose servant he once was: "I can still hear his 'Song of the Plane.'" Later, in Bern, he had seen Hebbel's *Maria Magdalene*, which strongly reminded him of Schiller's *Intrigue and Love*. Why was such an interesting play so rarely performed? He tells me the plot in great detail.

On contemporary poetry: "Do you not think that the current poets have an overly painterly sensibility? They are downright afraid to show their feelings. And so instead they search for original images. But do images alone comprise a good poem? Is it not feelings that give every poem its heartbeat?"

At the St. Gallen station restaurant: "I love hearing the tinkle of the cash register, the clattering of plates, and the bright ring of glasses. It sounds like an orchestra of coziness." In the last weeks he reread Marlitt's *In the Counselor's House* and the novel *In the Corner Window* by the adventurer Friedrich Gerstäcker; though his characters are cardboard cutouts, he is a thrilling storyteller. Robert Walser never had his own library—at most a stack of cheap paperbacks. What need was there for more? "Every place in the world is haunted by stories. In Bern I lived for a little while with a nice milliner at Kramgasse 19; the house once belonged to the lordly von Hallwyl family. But one would be wrong to think that Bern is always so cozy. On the contrary. There are spooks and ghosts all over. That is why I moved so often. Many rooms had something uncanny about them."

A few minutes before the train leaves I confess: "Don't be angry with me, Herr Walser! I was the one who had the head doctor ask whether you didn't want to live in a nicer ward!" Robert: "Why should I live in some finer ward? Didn't you remain a private, without the pretensions of an officer? Look, I am a kind of private as well, and so I wish to remain. I have as little desire to be an officer as you. I wish to live with the people and to disappear with them. That is the proper thing for me."

August 12, 1945

THE ATOM BOMB has been invented—the World War is over. After some stormy days, when the wind whistled through the trees at a hundred kilometers an hour, it has grown quieter again. Veil-thin fog lies over Lake Zürich as I drive to the train station.

I nestle into a nonsmoking corner of the express train and begin to read. In Winterthur a mother squeezes in with her little daughter, fat as a stuffed goose. She turns the quiet compartment into a nursery, full of self-importance, as if she is the center of the world. A doll is planted on the seat cushion, the girl's hair dressed, breakfast unwrapped with a great rustling of paper, her fat backside ostentatiously turned toward me, blocking my view.

Herisau. Robert waves from afar. He asks what I have planned. I: "Nothing." And so he sets the course himself. The sun has broken through; the roar of church bells accompanies us as we march through Gossau. Paradisiacal richness: apples upon apples, pears upon pears hang from the branches; grazing cows; Sunday morning peace. After Arnegg we turn south on meadow paths. Once we come upon a farmstead. An Appenzell mountain dog nips at our heels. A peasant woman stands at the door, but does not return our greeting. I say: "It seems to me that people here are less friendly than in Appenzell Outer Rhodes." Robert: "Not less friendly, just more reserved. We are in the Fürstenwald, which is Catholic." Suddenly the path ends. Robert: "We misunderstood the dog. He wanted to warn us that the field is private property. By the way, have you noticed that dogs nowadays are much quieter than they used to be, as if electricity, the telephone, the radio and such robbed them of speech?" I: "Shall we slip away?" Robert, stopping and waving the idea off with his umbrella like a conductor: "But, but—what are you, a defeatist?" He strikes a dramatic pose and quotes from Georg Büchner's *Danton*: "I see a great disaster overwhelming France. It is dictatorship, it has torn off its veil, it holds its head high, it tramples over corpses ..."*

We turn into a fir wood but after a few minutes we come to

* From *Danton's Death*, translated by Howard Brenton.

a boggy slope. We can hear a stream gurgling at the bottom. Robert: "Well I'll be damned—are we supposed to break our necks?... Forth to the light!" We end up in potato and wheat fields and have to climb over several tangles of barbed wire. As we rest, he says: "It is fitting, in light of what we've just survived, to remember Goncharov's *The Precipice* and Dostoevsky's *Demons*. I ask you therefore to listen with reverence: 'What else should I do here? Is it not all indifferent? I will become a citizen of Uri and live in the gorge until the end of my days.'"

I have never seen Robert's vagabond side so clearly as on this morning; he is as high-spirited as I have ever seen him. Trousers rolled, he catches a scent, gauges the height of the sun, and grasps my arm, as a troop of farmers comes into view: "Look lively, so we don't run into them!" Although he has never been in this area, he does not swerve. We dig into ham and beer at the restaurant Tannenberg. Tasty, but overpriced; a greedy waitress ... Land of cows, land of flies. We reach Engelburg just at midday, where the proprietress sets massive cutlets and plates of beans in front of us. A few villagers come in with guns and sashes, plumes and cornucopia. They are headed to a neighborly shooting match. On the way to Abtwil we talk of Carl Spitteler. Robert: "I see him more and more as an alienist, anointed to rule as a little god over fools. That is how Spitteler seems to me. There's something impressive, but also something offensive about it. One doesn't just slip into a position like his without arrogance or pride ... And by the way I never think of Spitteler when I think of writers. Among the Swiss it is almost always Keller with *Green Henry* and Meyer with *Jürg Jenatsch* who come to mind. Those were two democrats and storytellers whose like has been seen in this land neither before nor since." I: "And Gotthelf?" Robert: "Madame George Sand was enchanted by him; I prefer other gods."

He mentions what a miserable experience he has had with

Messieurs les éditeurs since leaving Berlin. He had to practically force his things on them. He simply wasn't in fashion. Almost everyone is a slave to fashion. Was it not a troubling spectacle to see certain publishers turning up in London before the victory bells had even stopped ringing, for fear of finding the cupboard bare at home? A little more idealism and a little less salesmanship would do them good, in his opinion.

Conversation about the married writers Efraim and Fega Frisch; Efraim: dramaturge at Reinhardt and editor of the magazine *Der Neue Merkur,* to which Robert Walser occasionally contributed; Fega: the sensitive translator of nearly fifty Russian *chefs d'oeuvre.* Robert tells me that Fega once invited him to tea when her husband was out of town. When they wanted to go out together after tea, he had offered his services to put on her shoes: "But she rejected my offer with charming tact."

In Herisau Robert draws his umbrella and points to the station restaurant: "*En avant*—to beer and twilight!" During a conversation about the defeated Germany, groaning from its wounds, he says, "May the Germans finally learn not to mess around with geniuses in politics! Their damned weakness for romanticism has completely ruined them. They always want to show the world what clever, unusually capable fellows they are. As if politics had anything to do with genius! Just look at that jovial cigar smoker Churchill! One can just as easily picture him sitting in a pub as at home in an armchair. He lacks all affectation and neurasthenia. And yet he too is a genius and saved much and many without any great fanfare. Doing the right thing, the rational thing, with energy: therein lies genius, and it is only in this way that Germany—and Europe with it—can avoid falling into the abyss."

September 23, 1945

RAINY MOUSE-GRAY SKY. The porter forgot to tell Robert of
my telephone call. Now he comes toward me at a brisk pace, his
battered hat in hand, and says: "What an unexpected pleasure!"

We trot through puddly fields toward Flawil. He comments
that he often welcomes rain. It makes the colors and scents more
intense, and under an umbrella one can feel quite at home.

At *Krone* in Flawil mighty platters of vegetables and meat are
placed before us, including a little plate of whipped cream at the
end. Since we are in cider heaven, we do the honors with the
newest batch. During the meal Robert says:

"You asked me last time about the patient A. D., whose
nephew you know. You had just left when I remembered him.
He died in our asylum about a year and a half ago. We called
him the 'Gold Uncle.' I think he spent quite a while in America,
on a farm or someplace. In any case, he told tales of secret riches
that he was expecting from there. Once a dignified older lady
visited him. Sabine was her name, and that's just how she looked:
like a character from a Gottfried Keller legend. This A. D. was
a terrible eater, by the way. Always as ravenous as a wolf. Once
I watched him pour a whole saltcellar on his food. I felt quite
sick as I watched him choking everything down in such a hurry.
He vomited afterwards, usually. He must have been dyspeptic."

On the way to Gossau: "I still have to tell you how quickly I
wrote *The Assistant*. As you know, the Scherl Verlag invited me
to take part in a novel contest. Well, why not? But the only thing
that occurred to me was my work experience in Wädenswil. So
I wrote it out immediately, and in a fair copy, no less. I was
finished in six weeks." I tell Robert that a native Wädenswiler
assured me that he recognized every pub and every character. An

advertising clock made by the inventor Tobler can still be seen in one of the train stations in the Zürich uplands, in Bäretswil, I think. Robert says: "After his bankruptcy I saw Tobler a few more times in Bern. He was a hot-tempered man, his wife a tall, silent Winterthurian." I: "Where does *The Tanners* take place?" Robert: "In Zürich and in the little Bernese township of Täuffelen, where my sister worked for a few years as a teacher, before she went to Livorno to work as a governess for seven years, and then to Bellelay, where she taught language lessons for nearly three decades. How often I stayed with her in Täuffelen and later in Bellelay!"

Finally: "I think that it is a fundamental problem of new Swiss literature that our authors so ostentatiously tout their own people as sweet and kindly, as if everyone here were a reformer like Pestalozzi. The unearned sense of security that our generation has enjoyed since the turn of the century has produced an authorial pedantry that I sometimes find downright repulsive. Every demon is beaten to death. How different Gottfried Keller was! I am convinced that he also had a villain inside him. The character Max Wohlwend was *him*. Without internal darkness an artist remains a half-formed thing, a scentless greenhouse plant. And the do-gooders we've had since Keller and Meyer are so dull!"

December 30, 1945

DRIVE TO RORSCHACH, where we wander through the fishing village of Staad, which smells of freshly baked bread, toward the Buchberg. In Buchen the singing of the congregation wafts from the church. Lonely the streets, lonely the homesteads, with bluish wisps of smoke curling from their chimneys. As we approach Schloss Greifenstein, a castle the mayor Vadian had built on the Buchberg for his daughter in the sixteenth century, Robert stops, rapt. I tell him that my friend the painter Charles Hug lives with his wife Renée in the neighboring farmhouse. I speak a bit louder than usual, in the hope that the two might hear us. After a few meters I turn to look back. Right: Renée looks out and waves to us. She calls out that Charles is ill. Would we like to visit him? Robert hustles me onward: "No, no, we mustn't let ourselves be detained!" How to conquer his unsociability? I say: "Let us just pay the sick man a brief visit! It would be impolite not to at least shake his hand." Reluctantly, Robert yields. Charles comes to meet us in the doorway in a dressing gown, his face yellow and wrinkled. I am startled by his beleaguered appearance; from afar he reminds me of Toulouse-Lautrec. He draws us into the warm parlor, where a Christmas tree slumbers. Renée brings coffee and fresh croissants. We look at Charles's pen drawings for Flaubert's *Sentimental Education*; Robert gradually loses his inhibitions in the companionable conversation and proves himself strikingly well versed in Flaubert's cast of characters. Charles fetches a few new oil paintings from his studio—delicate impressions of Lake Constance: dove-gray sky and dove-gray water. One can't tell where either ends or begins. I see that he has made great strides working with the nuances of color. We take a tour of the charming dwelling, and then say good-bye ...

When the house lies behind us and we are alone again, Robert stops and laughs: "Wasn't that charming? That warm parlor with the glittering tree and the candles! Those crispy pastries, as if they were imported straight from Paris!"

I ask him why he didn't go to Paris after Berlin. "To Paris? *Jamais*! I never would have dared to go where Balzac, Flaubert,

Maupassant, and Stendhal worked so inimitably. Never, never! After the Berlin debacle, the only right thing for me was to retreat to my homeland." Then after a brief silence: "I am not so dumb that I cannot take a critical survey of my own talent. Oh, who could ever compose as effortlessly as Gottfried Keller! He never wrote a superfluous line. Everything set down deliberately and judiciously, as it should be."

Robert is once again enraptured by the beauty of the Buchberg, which sits in the landscape with its vineyards like a good-natured whale. Heiden and Wolfhalden greet us with a light sheen of snow. In Rheineck we eat jugged hare in the hotel Hecht. Without any Buchberger wine, sadly; the red Neuenburger that we order isn't much good: "*vin fédéral.*" Robert tells me how once when he, Max Slevogt, Count Leopold von Kalckreuth, and Bruno Cassirer were sitting together, Slevogt made fun of Walser's flops. Robert should become a Stendhalian, he said. His books bored people. "What could I say? I sat there in all my failure and had to agree with him." Shortly thereafter: "One day I received from Albin Zollinger a copy of *Die Zeit*, the magazine he edited, which contained his review of *The Assistant*. Apparently he didn't consider the fact that the issue also contained an equally robust paean to another, rather insignificant, writer. Was Zollinger trying to imply: 'Don't take Walser too seriously! He is a little pipsqueak. There are others just as good as he.' Yes, that is how editors are. Like power-hungry boa constrictors they coil around the bodies of authors, squeezing and suffocating them however they want."

We duck into a dark beer cellar in St. Gallen. Robert says: "Curious how beer and twilight can wash away all burdens." We say good-bye in a wild flurry of snow.

July 17, 1946

AFTER A CRASHING thunderstorm in the night, morning sails in with a bright blue sky and long, fishlike Föhn clouds. Jubilant youths board the train on a class trip. Robert declines my suggestion to continue by train to Urnäsch and from there climb the Hundwilerhöhe: "No, let us do everything on foot!" He points to a green hilltop to the south. To me it looks impossibly far. But he must have his way. He strikes out at an almost tempestuous pace. His pants are a bit too long; he explains that they were his brother Karl's. Down into a gorge! There is an old mule track with a wire to hold on our right-hand side, which leads steeply downward. I propose a swim in the river that flows moss-green beneath us; and I tell him I wouldn't say no to a little snack, either. Robert parries my suggestion with a gesture of horror and declaims with both irony and pathos: "Those who seek victory do not rest!" Upward on the other side, then! He climbs up like a cat. Then past scattered cottage gardens, past strongly scented meadows, woods and more woods ...

We get into a long discussion on the following subject, which I raised: The attractive young daughter of some married friends of mine has come under the influence of a nasty fellow; I occasionally see them together in a cafe. I have heard many bad things about this brutal and unkempt-looking youth, who is said to have hypnotic powers. Supposedly he uses these powers to prey on the young. People gossip and claim that he has led the daughter of my friend to drink, and brings her along late at night to bars where improper things occur. So the problem is: Should I make the father (the mother is ill and must be spared) aware of the danger his daughter is in, or should I remain silent? Robert considers the issue thoroughly and inquires spiritedly into the particulars. Then he says: "I advise you in friendship to take no action. You will only expose yourself to unpleasantness. Perhaps people will suspect you of gossip, jealousy, and small-minded moralistic snooping. What is this girl to you! The affair, even if it ends in unhappiness, is a school of experience for the naive creature. One must have faith in life and in people that such moments of danger will awaken their strengths. Those who fall can also rise ... No, no, in your place I would stay nice and quiet!" I: "I admit: I will probably get nothing but unpleasantness from an intervention. But it is not a matter of my peace of mind; it is a matter of the girl, who is too good for this bastard. According to my understanding of the duty of friendship, I am obliged to tell her father." Robert: "There is no such thing as the duty of friendship. There is only friendship, free and without bonds. Why are you getting involved in affairs that are the responsibility only of the father and mother?" I: "I feel differently than you, quite frankly. If a friend fell next to me in battle, I would care for him without a second's hesitation, no matter what." Robert: "That too is wrong. Your duty would be to care only for victory, to fight onward and to win the battle. One must not lose sight of the greater goal for personal reasons. Those who want to win must also be able to face sacrifice."

Robert elaborates on his idiosyncratic ideas until we reach the hill. He tells me of a beauty from Biel whom he saw occasionally in Zürich. Her life had been ruined by an abortion. But she had made many men happy with her charms. There must also be ways of life that are not normal, but that develop on byways—peculiar fates. One must not tinker with nature simply because it is inscrutable.

A morning snack on the Hundwilerhöhe, where Robert once came with his sister Lisa, though on the easier route up from the Zürchermühle. Eyes shining, he enjoys the dramatic illumination of the dark, towering clouds, and the light gray flakes that roll down from the Säntis massif. He talks of Gerhart Hauptmann, who fell into the hands of the Russians in Agnetendorf and died there a month and a half later, probably of grief over the tragedy of his homeland. Robert had occasionally encountered him in Berlin. But later he got the impression that his mind and heart had fallen asleep on the "pillow of sensuality." "Wary generosity always pays off in the end. One must only be able to wait for the payment." When we leave the inn, the sky is an inky black. Single drops of rain fall, heavy as lead. We walk south along the ridge. A beautiful herd of cows is camped peacefully on the "oxen hill"; everything about them breathes calm, satiety, contentment. To be so content, for once ...! Down to the valley through woods and herds of young bulls. It's as if the rain isn't fast enough to follow us. Just after noon we stand, fairly dry, on the street, from which it is not far to Appenzell. Nonetheless, we set out toward Hundwil. An hour later we arrive at the village center. On the way, Robert expresses his astonishment that after *Martin Salander*, whose first chapter he greatly admires, Gottfried Keller wrote no more. Probably he was emotionally exhausted. We settle down at the *Bären* for veal with mushroom sauce, *Rösti*, beans, and caramel crème. Nearby, a group of holidaymakers gently sings "In Aargäu warr two loverss"; a few village children pass by on the street with accordions. The littlest one wears a long veil of St. Gallen lace on her back like a bride. We sit for nearly two hours. A doctor comes and uses a syringe on a guest in the next room who is suffering from a middle ear infection. His manner suggests that the five francs he was paid doesn't afford him the time to mess around.

I tell Robert about a journalist who is the pet brownnoser in a large editorial office. He tells them whatever they want to hear. A fellow without a single idealistic impulse, miserly and spiritless. He pulls sandwiches out of his leather briefcase during the most moving scenes in a play or film and chews them laboriously. Though he comes from a well-to-do family, they are ashamed to buy the paper in which he writes his lukewarm articles. He has the secretary send it to them. When his own father died he asked to cover the funeral. The editors gave him the assignment, but had enough of a sense of humor not to pay him for the piece. He's a character who belongs in a Molière play, dressed in an old-fashioned black jacket, as if he worked in some shabby counting house. Robert asks: "Have you noticed that nearly all misers live to be old as the hills? It's as if even death dreads them."

On the hike back we discuss the countercriticisms levied at me by a novelist after my negative review of him appeared in a magazine. Robert advises: "Laugh and say nothing, that is the best thing to do in such a situation. One must be able to bear a bit of a stink."

December 29, 1946

BONE-RATTLING CHILL; SOME twenty centimeters of snow on the ground. We nearly have to run to keep warm, as Robert wears no coat. The silvery-gray mood of the morning pleases him. Only once is he combative, when a dog comes out of a farmstead and circles us, barking loudly. Robert chases him a few steps and yells: "You little devil, you, I'll teach you to leave us in peace!"

Two hours later we reach Niederteufen, where we order *café complet* at a bakery. The baker's wife is in church. Giggling, her young daughter prepares our breakfast with a half-witted maid. Robert delights in the fresh white raisin bread; he laps up the plum butter like a cat. It took some effort to get him to Teufen; more than once he wanted to turn toward St. Gallen. Now, however, he speaks unprompted of his grandfather Johann Ulrich Walser, who was born here and had fourteen children. During the Baden uprisings, many revolutionary tracts were printed in his Liestal printing shop and smuggled across the Rhine under the cover of night.

On the road between Teufen and Speicher, the youth of the village are amusing themselves on sleds and skis. Later it grows very quiet and foggy. "Russian," Robert says. "Look out, we're heading for desolate waters!" He tells me that Biel produces the most disparate writers—some on the far left of the political spectrum, others on the far right. One was even tried for treason: "This led me to observe that the extremes of the spectrum tend to meet, and are in fact as alike as siblings." For him personally, Biel had been a place of recuperation, so to speak, where he had gathered his strength after the metropolitan stresses and strains of Berlin. He had returned with only a few francs in his pocket, a mocked man, an unsuccessful author, and had used his first paycheck from his job as a bank apprentice to amass a library of cheap paperback classics, and had played minor roles in the dramatic society. But he flares up, as if bitten by a snake, when I say: "But how can you claim to be unsuccessful? Is success measured by the weight of the books produced by an author? How many people there are who still speak of your work with the greatest enthusiasm!" He cries out despairingly into the fog: "Quiet, quiet! How can you say something like that! Do you really think I believe your society lies?" A rider gallops past on a stout horse, the village veterinarian perhaps, then disappears like a phantom. I soothe Robert, and we begin to speak of the fundamental problem of writers—that they always wish to correct their fellow man. It is only through flaws that a character attains depth, Robert opines, then adds that people have dumped buckets of cheap advice on him personally. As we eat lunch in Appenzellerhof in Speicher, he remarks: "What a shame that Gottfried Keller had to waste away in a conventional bourgeois house on Zeltweg, dying like a mouse in a trap!" At which I can't help interjecting: "Look, Herr Walser, now you too are schoolmastering a bit, in the old Swiss fashion!" Smiling, he admits: "Yes, it's true. But it can't hurt Keller anymore."

May 26, 1947

IN GOSSAU WE encounter a field processional; the red vestments of the acolytes gleam like geraniums. We want to go to Oberbüren, where Robert has never been. He insists that we not stray from the wide road. Dozens of cars, bicycles, and motorbikes flash by, dangerously close. But he remains unperturbed, and, as evidence that loyalty is rewarded and disloyalty punished, he tells me the story of *Eugénie Grandet*, by Balzac. In the end he agrees to take a byway. At my suggestion we choose the path to the right through the woods, but Robert warns: "The right way often leads to wrong, and the wrong way to right."

Oberbüren lies nestled in a basket of trees. On a door we read the following motto:

> Good luck and bad luck
> Make no ado
> Both will pass
> As will you.

Breakfast: Tilsit cheese, butter, milky coffee, beer. The proprietress as ascetic, gaunt and serious as St. Nicholas of Flüe. She sits at the next table counting under her breath, while the maid takes care, with motherly concern, that we get enough to eat. We hear prayers droning from the kitchen; apparently some sect is holding a meeting in the house ... I tell Robert that on Whit Monday I sat directly behind Thomas Mann at the opening night of Strindberg's *Dream Play*. I was struck by his long, pointy nose and his full head of ungrayed hair. Robert: "It's the health of success. How many are driven to an early grave by failure! Since childhood Thomas Mann had it all: bourgeois calm, security, a happy family, recognition. Even immigration couldn't upset him. On foreign soil he wrote diligently, like a clerk in an office; thus the Joseph novels, which feel dry and labored, are not nearly as good as his astonishing early works. In the later works one senses the stale indoor air, and that's the way their maker looks too, like someone who has always sat diligently behind his desk with the account books. But his bourgeois orderliness and his almost scientific effort to put every detail in the right place deserve some respect."

Then, as we rest by some trees, laden with fruit: "The trees have it good. They can bear fruit every year." Onward! Niederwil; the pastor, greeting us warmly, marches with the village band to a festival in Flawil. We turn back onto the motorway, which shimmers like tin in the midday heat; a strip of tar splits it down the middle like a dirty black brook. Robert's face reddens in the sun like a tomato. But he smiles at me encouragingly: "It would be nice to continue on like this into the night, right in step with each other."

Gossau. We hesitate before the wide façade of an inn. A villager passes by and, without turning his head (probably afraid the staff or owner will see him scaring off customers), says: "Go to the Krone!" So we do, and are indeed rewarded with a lavish meal: meat broth, tender schnitzel topped with a fried egg, beans, carrots, noodles, salad, and frozen meringues, accompanied, according to Robert's express wish, by a Spanish red wine. At the next table, the potbellied proprietor, who has a lame leg, is explaining to other guests how to cook a turkey: how one must remove the nerves and carefully prepare the four types of meat. As in every métier, here too we enjoy his practical knowledge, and the care that resonates even in his seemingly cool tone. Conversation about the recently deceased Charles Ferdinand Ramuz. Robert admits that he was the most distinctive writer in Western Switzerland. But he finds his regionalism antiquated, and sometimes forced. Nowadays, art must turn its eye toward humanity as a whole, rather than on the peasantry of one's homeland, which already found an unparalleled chronicler in Gotthelf. I confess my admiration for the wistful aristocratism for Count Eduard von Keyserling, whose *Harmony* and *Gay Hearts* I recently read. Did Robert ever meet him in person? "Yes, I saw him sometimes in Munich at Café Stephanie, where he sat almost every day in proud solitude over a little glass of cognac, nearly blind, an unbustling person surrounded by bustlers, all of whom wanted only to make a career for themselves as quickly as possible. He seemed to me like a lion *par exellence*." In response to my inquiring look, he explains: "The lion is king of his kingdom. A king on the verge of extinction. Such a creature was Eduard von Keyserling." Robert finds the grandeur of his prose mesmerizing: "The true masters have no need to make a show of being masters. They simply are—*basta!*"

On our evening walk Robert remarks on the clergy of today: "I am struck by how many pastors act as if they are still living in the time of Calvin, Zwingli, or Bullinger. They scramble after an asceticism whose necessity they themselves no longer understand. But they believe they owe it to tradition, even though they have far more important things to do nowadays." I: "For example?" Robert: "Talk less of God and act more in accordance with God."

November 3, 1947

SOOT-BLACK SKY. "HAVE you eaten breakfast?" "No, you?" "Me neither!" "Very well, then: first the body, then the other thing." We have no luck at the poorly lit train station. The strapping waitress regrets that she cannot offer us coffee: there is no milk. And so we walk through the silent village. I ask in a bakery if they can feed us. It smells of fresh bread; in fact the baker is sliding a few loaves into the mouth of the oven with a long wooden paddle. No, there's no breakfast today, he answers, his wife is visiting relatives. Bad luck! The third try, at a pub, succeeds. But the breakfast is bad and expensive, the young waitress grumpy. Robert likewise.

A silent hike to Oberberg Schloss, which lies perched on a hill. The honey-yellow flames of the fruit trees seem to soothe Robert a little. We enter the castle, which was built in the mid-thirteenth century and has been collectively owned since 1924. Without being asked, the maid opens the doors to the chapel, the arms room, the torture chamber, and the bedroom, where Robert tenderly strokes the calico drapery of the canopy bed. I help her carry the kettle into the kitchen. Robert likes the warm dining room, but the little waitress fiddles with matches near our table, making him nervous. And so we continue on. It begins to pour, it's as if the sky is trying to whip the earth with water. Robert has an umbrella, I have a shabby coat. We zigzag through the fields and woods, across a ravine and through Abtwil to Engelburg. Sometimes Robert stops and marvels, murmuring incomprehensibly, at the rust-red foliage. In front of a villa with a little tower I remark: "That could be the villa in *The Assistant*!" Astounded, he answers: "It really is the same style. That is just how Villa Abenstern in Wädenswil looked when I was there as an assistant, bustling to and fro."

Since it rains harder and harder, such that we now look like drowned cats, I suggest that we should take the tram at the edge of St. Gallen. Robert, however, thinks we must persevere. Very well! Eventually we end up, drenched, in the third-class station restaurant and hide ourselves in a corner, so that no one will notice the ponds that are forming at our feet. They have jugged hare. Robert grins. Over dessert I mention that the Nobel Peace Prize has been awarded to the Quakers. He asks: "Did you know that their leader, the itinerant preacher William Penn, founded the state of Pennsylvania three hundred years ago and dreamed of a League of Nations? Zschokke writes about him in a pretty novella." Back then, in Zschokke's day, people still knew how to write graceful novellas: "Today writers terrorize readers with fat, boring books. It is an unsavory sign of the times that literature has become so imperialistic. Before, it was modest, sweet-natured. Now it has pretensions to power. It sees the people as its subjects. This is an unhealthy development."

Near evening, he wants to return to Herisau on foot. He then realizes, however, that returning to the asylum looking like a waterfall might arouse a disagreeable fuss. So we defect to the train. It is only in the compartment that I learn the reason for his ill humor: from now on I am only allowed to visit on Sundays. On weekdays, he must work like the rest of the residents. I: "The head doctor told me explicitly that I could go walking with you whenever we like!" Robert, serious and firm: "The head doctor! *Je m'en fiche.* It is not only the doctor I care about. I must also consider the patients. Can't you understand that as a person of privilege, I would play an indelicate role?"

April 4, 1948

THE MEADOWS SPARKLE like jewels in the barely melted snow, as we walk toward Degersheim. We come to speak of Max Brod, who is currently staying in Zürich. Robert remembers that in 1919 his face appeared next to Brod's in a Leipzig newspaper. I tell him how the chief clerk, under whom Franz Kafka worked at the Worker's Accident Insurance Institute, had compared Kafka to the dreamers in Walser's books, and how Kafka had recommended *The Tanners* to his literary-minded boss. Kafka had also spoken enthusiastically of *Jakob von Gunten*, and had read some of Walser's Berlin stories aloud to Max Brod, especially "Mountain Halls," whose lines "The publican is making his watchful bouncer rounds through the establishment. He sees to decorum and proper behavior. Do pay the place a visit, why don't you, eh?"* in particular he read with a connoisseur's élan. But Robert remarks dryly that there are more exciting things to read in Prague than Walserian trifles. Prague had a famous university by the fourteenth century, and was long a citadel of German culture. It had only lost prominence under the unthinkable narrow-mindedness of National Socialist politics. He himself had never been to Prague, but he recalls that around 920 A.D. members of a Czech nationalist group strangled the Bohemian princess Ludmilla with the help of her stepdaughter Dragomir's treachery. There were, by the way, also charming murderesses in world history. Here he calls my attention to Jan Neruda, founder of the Czech *feuilleton*, whose tales of Prague he had long ago encountered in a paperback edition, and which he found as cozy as Dickens's stories.

On byways we turn into the woods. It smells of moist earth and spring. We climb through undergrowth up a slope that gets

---

* From *Berlin Stories*, translated by Susan Bernofsky.

steeper and steeper until we stand on a meadow carpeted with deep blue gentian and wasp-yellow primroses. Following the laborious path of a magpie, Robert wants to climb yet higher. Finally, thorny hedges block any further progress. Robert agrees with my remark: "We should be cleverer than Hitler and beat a retreat while we still can!" In a quarter of an hour we are standing before the inn Zum Fuchsacker. An elderly couple brings us butter, cheese, and coffee. A black and yellow cat jumps up on the bench and rubs itself fawningly against our knees. This attracts a fox terrier, who sits on its hind legs and likewise begs for a snack. Later, some old relatives of the proprietors come into the room—a farmer and his wife with sharply etched, canny Appenzell faces. The man recounts how his irritated appendix had suddenly been cured with an ointment from a natural healer. The landlord sits with us and talks of his experiences hunting badgers. Little dogs often risk their lives when they try to pull the animals, who can weigh up to half a hundredweight, out of their dens. The farmer's wife adds that once a hunchbacked badger had hidden in such a den. It was next to impossible to pull him out.

Finally we tear ourselves away from this homey circle to roam for another hour in the woods before eating lunch at Sternen in Degersheim. Robert orders veal with mushroom cream sauce, *Rösti*, and meringues. On the way home we talk about our military experiences. Robert says: "I always had to report for duty in Bern. Often we were posted to Jura, and once to St. Maurice and into the Val Mesolina. While my comrades were snoring, I read over proofs of *The Life of a Poet* in a barn by the dim light of an oil lamp. That must have been 1918." I remark: "But for chance, you could been a French writer! Don't people in Biel speak both French and German?" Robert: "That's right; in the neighboring town of Leubringen or Evilard, French is actually dominant.

But it never occurred to me to write in two languages. It cost me enough trouble to write in proper German. Yes, a singer at the Bern Stadttheater, to whom I gave one of my books, had the impertinence to give me the book back with the words: 'Learn German before you try to write stories!'"

January 23, 1949

A SEGANTINI SKY. The train to Appenzell is filled with hordes of skiers. The snow twinkles, bright as a mirror, in the morning light. Robert at the train station in a new gray hat. He talks of Ernst Zahn's eighty-second birthday, which is tomorrow, and expresses admiration of his professional abilities, although he finds his books too narrowly tailored to local interests. But how much fatherly dignity Zahn must have possessed, even in his youth, that the skeptical Urians voted him town councilor, then judge of the criminal court, then president of the cantonal council! Then he refers to the hundredth birthday of August Strindberg, which was celebrated yesterday. Twenty years or so ago at the Schänzli Theater in Bern he had seen Gertrud Eysoldt in his *Miss Julie*. What a nasty play! In it, a footman seduces a lady of the castle. "I coulda killt the bastard!" Strindberg was a woman-killer, just like that footman. Conceited and diabolical. He was always full of hatred. The following day Robert had seen Wedekind's *Earth Spirit*. There was a different writer entirely—more human, nobler. But women would have taken lascivious revenge on Strindberg. Just as he wanted to kill women, they would have killed him in the end. One cannot live and write without love and go unpunished. I tell Robert that in the summer of 1947 I spent some time with Gertrud Eysoldt: "She received me in a boarding house on Dufourstrasse. A graceful, white-haired lady, seventy-seven years old. She described how back then in Bern she had left a note in your room, hoping you would see it. You then went to a restaurant where she was sitting with several actors, and invited her for a walk. She said she would never forget the charming Swiss-Gallic way you pointed out the city's hidden beauty. Your way of hearkening to the esoteric joys of life, and the mischievous way you have of coming to terms with mankind's foibles always captivated her. You must have been following the prescription a poet once gave for lovers: 'Be modest and you'll win!'" Silence. Then Robert asks me how Frau Eysoldt weathered the war. "She said that neither the First nor the Second World War could shake her. In fact she had been surprised by the Russians in Silesia and lost all her property, so to speak. But she continued: 'My home was and is the realm between heaven and earth. I never put much stock in external possessions, though I was able to acquire many valuable things, exquisite works of art. After the war, when I lived in Bavaria in the direst poverty and many days didn't know what I would get to eat, I was allowed to use the library of the painter Friedrich Kaulbach. There I read Plutarch, Herodotus, Marcus Aurelius, Plato, Laozi, and other Chinese sages, and I felt better and more at ease than I ever did among riches. I ate my dry bread crusts almost as if they were something holy.'" Robert: "Yes, it is good when hardship forces one back to the simple things. How much ballast was swept away by the war, and how much space it has made for the beautiful to grow within us again!" I: "We also talked of politics, Gertrud Eysoldt and I. She said she had never understood how people could claim politics was unclean. People had simply made it unclean. At bottom, politics was absolutely necessary to preserve the freedom of the individual. One of its primary goals must be to make people prosperous, so that they possess the things that they need. Things, yes—but it must not go so far that things take possession of people. Therefore politics mustn't allow wealth. For wealth can enslave people, and that is the worst thing of all." Robert: "Even in Berlin I admired Frau Eysoldt as an actress." I: "Do you know how she got her start with Max Reinhardt? She told me herself. When she came to Berlin, Reinhardt cast her in Strindberg's one-act *The Stronger*. Originally an attractive colleague was meant to play the role. But she was so hopelessly dumb that she was replaced by Gertrud Eysoldt. Her character didn't have a single line. But her gestures and facial expressions made such an impression on Reinhardt that he cast her soon afterward as Hauptmann's Hannele and Oscar Wilde's Salome. That time in Zürich she also said to me: 'I belonged to the avant-garde from the very beginning. New shores, new oceans—that's what I longed for. That's why I was chosen by directors with a preference for modern, problematic female characters. Wedekind, Maeterlinck, Strindberg, Claudel. How I would love to experience the new art that is surely to come, great and radiant—probably from Asia! As for me, I am only fit to play a grandmother nowadays. But my heart has remained so shamelessly young!'" Robert: "There are artists who simply never age. Gertrud Eysoldt is one of them." I: "She sighed a bit at the fact that everyone around her was already dead: Carl Spitteler, Gerhart Hauptmann, Max Reinhardt. 'I cannot,' she said then in the salon of her boarding house, 'catch up if they are already in seventh heaven, and I'm still crawling around here below.' Anyway, she had no desire to leave the earth just yet, where life had so much to offer to those who turn toward the higher, purer things. Then she asked me: 'Do you remember the speech that Victor Hugo made for Voltaire's centenary? Wasn't it splendid? I have often recited it: Is there anything more manly or liberal? It has often occurred to me, by the way, that actors like to pay homage to femininity a bit, and actresses to masculinity. I myself am no exception.'" Robert: "Have you seen Frau Eysoldt since then?" I: "No. As it happens, she was less enchanted by Switzerland than most foreigners are. She admitted to me that it did not seem like a paradise to her. The Swiss didn't exude happiness, which was the essential thing, she said. Eating well had long since ceased to be her definition of paradise; our land lacked intellectual and spiritual nourishment. Her true homeland was wherever sorrow was bravely overcome, a place ruled by a fellowship of the good. This homeland, which had nothing to do with nationalism, could never be taken away. Often during the war she had gone to her mother's grave in search of peace. She had cried bitterly there. But when she saw how love continued to inspire faith in young hearts, how the earth continually renewed itself, how animals have the courage to exist by following their natural instincts, her mind had grown brighter again."

We talk for hours of this actress and of Robert's trips to the theater in Berlin. His memory is remarkable. He asks me if I saw Shakespeare's *All's Well That Ends Well* on New Year's Eve. When I answer "Yes!" it becomes clear that he remembers even the minor characters quite accurately. In fact he's never seen the play, only read it in Berlin … forty years ago or more. *Café complet* at the St. Gallen station restaurant. Then three large lagers, after which I suggest: "Shouldn't we take a little stroll through the city?" Robert, who feels safe and secure: "Why bother, really? Let us stay where we are and eat lunch!" Bernese *Rösti*, fried eggs, and meringues. Afterwards, a walk through the quiet, snow-covered alleys. When we see a young priest looking out of a cloister, Robert remarks: "He is homesick for the outside, we for the inside." An old woman with disorderly white hair grumbles from a house across the street about how some boys tormented a young cat. She won't stop ranting about them. One might almost think she was mad. Robert is not bothered, however. He peers into courtyards and gardens as if they're enchanted islands. We climb higher up the Freudenberg, past frozen ponds and into the snowy woods. "It's like a fairy tale," he whispers, laying his hand lightly on my arm.

April 15, 1949

HOT, SUMMERY GOOD Friday walk to Degersheim, where we celebrate Robert's seventy-first birthday by eating pike. Of a meadow strewn with buttercups and gentian he remarks: "Compared to nature, we are nothing but a bunch of bumblers!"

Since Bismarck's dismissal, German politics had become criminal. Kaiser Wilhelm II took every opportunity to pick on France. Since then there had been no greatness in Germany.

Robert thinks the current generation of writers is too mollycoddled. They cannot bear failure: "The offended person runs immediately to Mama 'public' and whines that he has been treated badly. Look at the faces of today's writers! You'll see the faces of some real villains and murders among them. Perhaps good people have no business in art at all. If the artist wants to produce something interesting, he must have a demon inside him. Angels don't make good artists."

"But where does the demon's spell begin and where does it end?" I ask. "Yes, the line is hard to see," he admits. "I experienced this with a comrade in the army," I tell him. With his short gray hair he looked almost like a convict. For the most part, he held himself apart from the other soldiers, and when we all went off to the pub after muster, he was usually to be seen sitting forlornly in front of his pallet, his round skull propped thoughtfully in his hands. Something pietistic, something willful emanated from this man. But for a long time I considered him a rather harmless, gentle soul, who inspired more pity than horror. Other than carpentry, climbing in the mountains, and his family, nothing interested him. As a soldier he did his duty well, and after taking a climbing course he even achieved the rank of private first class. As if by tacit agreement, everyone left him alone when we had free time, since most people instinctively sensed a certain asocial element in his character. In our unit he was neither popular nor unpopular. He was simply a zero, and perhaps I would have thought as little about him as everyone else, if I hadn't once, while we were out on watch together, had the occasion to catch a glimpse into his soul … It happened like this: I returned from patrol to the dusky camp in an almost lyrical mood. An indescribably beautiful Föhn evening was trembling over the land. The Sargans fortress lay amid huge dull chunks of rock that looked like the gray hides of elephants. The castle beyond the border, enthroned atop a hill in Liechtenstein, appeared in the violet light like a ghost castle; a hundred meters below, the little church, which looked as if it was built of toy building blocks, gazed up at it like a supplicant. The woods and wheat-yellow fields, the tall reeds and the stubbly meadows, over which two birds of prey hunted their rodent quarry, created the kind of mood one sees in the paintings of Albrecht Altdorfer. At this point the private pulled me out of my devotional mood and into a conversation about his profession. He told me of the many dangers one is exposed to in a mechanized workshop like his, and described how often he himself had come close to being maimed. He dashed off dozens of examples of how machines are not just useful to man, but that they also endeavor to shorten his life. With great precision he demonstrated the positions his colleagues in the carpenter's guild had been in at the instant an accident occurred. He showed me how at the moment of explosion a finger or hand was pulled into the machine, how a lath, as if shot from a crossbow, whizzed directly into the chest of a planer standing five meters away, and how an elderly father, who had come to watch his son work, had his head cut off by a saw through his own carelessness. The uncanny and astonishing thing was that this seemingly gentle private unfolded these horror stories with great humor. He savored every detail, and when he reached the climax of the accident, in each case he laughed as if recounting an anecdote from the theater. The proximity of death appeared to positively invigorate him. His otherwise stony features were enlivened with passion, his nut-brown eyes began to glow; with his right hand, which was missing a thumb, he traced the scenes that he described, almost elegantly. This dramatic conversation lasted over an hour. At the end I said to the man: 'You really would have been better suited for an executioner!' which he acknowledged with a smile that contained both sadness and something demonic." After this extreme experience, Robert turns the conversation to Dostoevsky's *Demons*. He reminds me that in his notes for the novel, the author had Prince Stavrogin prophesy: "I believe that in the end all people will turn into either angels or devils."

Penance Day 1949

CONVERSATION ABOUT THE suicide of the playwright Caesar von Arx. This prompts Robert to talk at length of the relationship between writers and society. In his view it is necessarily a contentious one: "When artists do not stand in opposition to society, they quickly flag. They must not allow themselves to be coddled by it, or they will feel themselves obliged to cling to the existing conditions. Never, not even in the times of my greatest poverty, would I have let myself be bought by society. Personal freedom was always more important to me." The beautiful autumn day leads us through lonely Toggenburg: past herds of cattle with bells ringing and trees bursting with fruit. Near midday we reach the Magdenau convent, which was given to the Cistercians in 1244 by the chamberlain of the church of St. Gallen, Rudolf Giel, and his wife. Robert looks curiously at the entrance to the "almsroom." A nun scurries past like a mouse, no sooner seen than gone. Robert reminds me that the encyclopedist Diderot—whose masterpiece *Rameau's Nephew*, about a cynical sluggard, was translated into German by Goethe at Schiller's suggestion—also wrote the successful novel *The Nun*, a bold, honest book about the trials of a beautiful nun. She was forced into a convent, cruelly tormented, and hounded with lesbian propositions. Robert speaks of the book, which he read in an edition with pornographic illustrations, with great respect.

Two kilometers or so below the convent, in a charming little valley, lies the Romanesque Bubental church, which still has its original pews. The painting and sculpture, on the other hand, are new, and not exactly tasteful. Next to the church is a sawmill. On the way, Robert stops before the marsh where the steward Christoph Lieber, a follower of the Abbey of St. Gallen during the Toggenburger Troubles, was put to death for his "Resistance in the Matter of the States." Lunch in Flawil. Back through the woods. Somewhat dulled by the opulent meal, Robert talks briefly of his roommate, an escaped Polish Jew. He's a raving epileptic who likes to boast of his successes. Robert keeps a cautious distance, as the Pole has the face of a criminal.

February 5, 1950

A MILD, EARLY spring Sunday bookended by moody days of storm and rain. In the morning we walk in the villa quarter of the Rosenberg, in the afternoon to "Drei Linden" and up the

Notkersegg hill—below us, sometimes swathed lightly in fog, St. Gallen, as always. In a pastry shop Robert rolls a misshapen cigarette. Since it isn't well tamped, it flares a bit when lit. The couple next to us begins to giggle; they apparently take Robert for an unworldly farmer. He tells me that now he sorts and unravels twine for the post office. But he is content with the work. He simply takes what comes.

Strange conversation about virtue and vice. Robert says: "People are much prouder of their vices than their virtues, particularly in youth. I myself was once that way, back in Zürich, when I consorted with all kinds of loose, impertinent fellows, when I quit positions for the sake of poetry, and wrote *Fritz Kocher's Essays*." I tell him that I saw an amateur production of Shakespeare's *Twelfth Night* in Wädenswil. "Wädenswil? I remember it fondly. You'll know it from *The Assistant*, where I also described my post as a clerk in an elastic factory in Winterthur. That only lasted a few weeks, though, since before I started in Wädenswil, I had to do eight weeks of rifle drills."

Later the conversation turns to Bern. Robert asks me who I know there. I name two or three people. I was there almost exclusively on military service. Who did Robert associate with in Bern? He turns to me and says a bit more softly: "With myself!"

July 23, 1950

WHEN I ARRIVE in Herisau on the usual train, Robert is not at the station. I am astonished. He's always so punctual! I circle the station buildings for half an hour. Then I call the asylum. An attendant says Robert left long ago. He cannot explain why we haven't yet met. More waiting. Then I set off for the asylum.

I read on a plaque that the local council resolved to construct it in April 1906. Arthur Schiess, owner of an embroidery factory, donated 800,000 francs. From his will: "It is a wonderful privilege, not to mention a distinguished duty, for those of property and wealth to render a good portion of their earnings back to the general public for works of humanity and social welfare."

I announce myself to the porter and sit down, smoking a cigarette, on a shaded bench in the garden. Shortly thereafter, a representative comes from the head doctor, Dr. Hans Steiner. He receives me in his lodgings. Three sweet children follow us, barefoot. Later we are joined by the doctor's wife, who relates with a laugh how I once described her in a newspaper as a "gentle air-raid marshal." Dr. Steiner says that Robert is an "easy" patient who does his allotted work scrupulously. He is also, however, one of the more unsociable residents. If one starts to talk to him about art, he immediately grows recalcitrant.

When the porter announces Robert's arrival, I go to meet him. I notice from the surly way he greets me (as we shake hands he pulls back a meter or so, as if I am a porcupine) that he's in a bad mood. He cannot understand how we missed each other. He says he was at the Herisau station at eight on the dot, but continued on to Gossau after a few minutes, thinking he had been told the wrong meeting place. From Gossau he ambled back to the asylum, figuring the day was a wash. I: "I arrived on the same train as always. But it was delayed a quarter of an hour." Robert, completely bewildered: "So I really didn't wait long enough?" I nod and suggest—by now it's half past ten—that we take a leisurely stroll through the village and eat there. But he won't hear of it. He wants to get out of Herisau—and go to Schwellbrunn. *All right.* As we walk along the lonesome, upward-meandering paths, we quickly find a conversation topic that catches Robert's interest: Korea. Robert: "You mean 'Don Correa'?" I: "No, I mean the war in Korea!" Robert: "Isn't 'Don Correa' a thousand times more interesting? Surely you know Gottfried Keller's charming story of the Portuguese naval hero, which so naturally marries the moralistic and liberal ideas?" Then he rages for half an hour with increasing intensity against America's intervention in Korea: "Have you seen their faces? They're the faces of gangsters, executioners: foolishly proud, arrogant, and predatory. What business do the Americans have with a civilized society's fight for freedom? Of course they will destroy everything with their ultramodern war machines, and they'll win. But afterward how will the capitalist beast be driven back into its cage? That is another, more protracted question. In any case, Washington isn't exactly full of the best and brightest."

Meanwhile it has grown intolerably hot. Deathly muggy. Our brisk tempo seems to have tired Robert. Suddenly he clams up and won't respond to anything I say. His face turns crimson. He wipes his brow nervously. I've taken off my jacket and tied it around my shoulders; he keeps his vest and jacket buttoned. Finally I say: "Shall we rest in the shade a moment?" But he interrupts and says gruffly: "Don't worry about me! *C'est mon affaire.* Everyone must be his own keeper." Onward, then! Up and down hills, through woods and meadows, finally along motorways. Robert slows the pace and sometimes stops crossly. I worry that he'll have a stroke. Finally it begins to rain. Lightly at first; the wind kicks up dust. Then in buckets. We leave our umbrellas closed and stand under the colossal shower. The rain splashes off our brows. Eventually we find ourselves sitting somewhere in Schwellbrun over *Rösti*, fried eggs, beer, and pastries. Robert gives me a conciliatory look and smiles. The thaw is brief, however. He categorically rejects my suggestion that we take the mail van: "What do we have feet for?" —Off we go, then! After a quarter of an hour it begins to pour again, now even more heavily than before. We're soon completely soaked, despite our umbrellas. I see the mail van approaching us from behind and timidly repeat my suggestion that we take it. Robert consents with a snarl. Finally, at the Herisau train station, his disposition grows less stormy. He shows a lively interest in Heinrich Mann's death, of which he was ignorant, and allows me to tell him the story of the bombing of Dresden, as I heard it from the mouth of Gerhart Hauptmann's widow and son Bruno.

A long handclasp at the station.

April 6, 1952

ROBERT IS SURLY and distraught when I suggest we continue to Rorschach by train. Probably he suspects some plan that could throw him off balance. We sit in the smoking compartment saying hardly a word. He rolls clumsy cigarettes and puffs nervously. Then we begin to walk toward Staad. The sand-gray early spring sky and the earth melt gently into each other at the edge of Lake Constance. No ships, no people. We climb up and down toward the hamlet of Buchen; children and adults are on their way to a confirmation ceremony. Bucolic Palm Sunday mood! This time Robert wants to leave the Buchberg on our left. The quiet woods are calling him. He roams in front of me between firs, beeches, and undergrowth like a dog on the hunt, coatless, head and shoulders bent forward, his hands hanging down, bluish-red with cold. Finally we end up in Wienacht-Tobel, a charming stop on the Rorschach–Heiden rack railway. In the hamlet we enjoy some sharp Appenzell cheese and coffee. The croaking proprietor, who suffers from a laryngeal tumor, takes part in the usual conversation about the weather, the grapevines, the high price of wood. Then onward to Heiden, where it begins to snow. At midday we slide back to Buchen over slippery hillsides. The snow now turns into rain, which gets heavier and heavier. As we pass an exquisite park estate above the city, Robert breathes: "Like an Eichendorffian fairy-tale castle!"

Lunch in Rorschach. Then to a pastry shop, where some adolescent rowdies are making a fearful din. At the harbor we take the wrong train due to my carelessness, and find ourselves heading to Romanshorn instead of St. Gallen. I declare the accident a piece of good luck, as the lonesome, reedy shore we ride along is now drenched with sun, and its palette of gray, yellow, and blue is a real marvel of color. But it arouses Robert's suspicion. Probably he suspects some intent behind the "accident." He relaxes only when we board the train to St. Gallen in Romanshorn and ride slowly home through meadows and fruit trees. I fall asleep from the overstimulation and only wake shortly before St. Gallen. At the station restaurant Robert begins to talk of C. F. Meyer: "You know I hold him in high regard, particularly his *Jürg Jenatsch*. But when his style grows craggy and crystallizes into something monumental, I find him strange. Language must remain fluid." Looking at a photograph of a successful but talentless artist: "Look at that face! No critic could expose his obtuseness as cruelly as his own face!" Shortly afterward, of a snobbish writer who is always trying to wangle connections to the men of the hour, and then boasts of his friendships in "good" society: "There is nothing stupider than intellectual arrogance. This man lets the light of others shine on him, because he himself does not shine."

Christmas 1952

"WHERE SHOULD WE go?" Robert asks at the Herisau station. It's raining: not hard, but persistently. The sky looks as if it's covered with a fine layer of coal dust. Robert stands coatless, umbrella in hand. We circle the station a few times. Then Robert swings around onto a road that leads south and upward. About a hundred meters later he suggests: "No, let's take the lower road!" We walk a little way. But then he turns around again and asks: "Do you really have no plan?" I reply: "No, none at all. I'll go where you like!" Eventually we find ourselves standing on the upper road again. He hesitates and says: "Perhaps the lower is the better one after all!" and so finally we start out toward the Engelburg. A sign points to another castle in Herisau. He tells me that there are two of them in the area, one of them not far from the asylum. Both have been restored, which he finds indiscreet: "It's a confession of our generation's failure. Why not let the past sink and molder? Aren't ruins more beautiful than something that's been patched up? These historicizing architects who dig for forgotten shadows and want to restore the old faces of medieval buildings in the name of piety would be better off making something new and original that we could all be proud of. One of them lives in Biel, a Czech. A slim little man with blue-black hair. He rebuilt the southern part of Erlach, which burned down in the First World War."

The rain increases. A motorist stops and offers us a ride. We thank him politely. Robert: "That has never happened to me before! But walking does one more good than driving. If laziness advances at its current pace, it won't be long before people don't need their legs at all."

Quiet in all the villages and alleyways. Only cats on the prowl. A child with a doll in its arms tells me proudly, in dialect: "The Chris'chile gave me a schoolbag!" The child is carrying it on its back.

On a barn hangs a poster from a theatrical society: "Anna Koch, the murderess of Gonten." Robert tells me that she threw her rival into a pond out of jealousy and was executed for it in 1849. The girl was so unwilling to die that she even struggled with the executioner as she was taken to be killed. People at the asylum occasionally speak of the murderess, but Robert doesn't feel personally able to judge her, as she acted in the heat of the moment, and from perhaps not ignoble impulses. He is a strict opponent of capital punishment in general; it implies a presumption that he detests. Later in the St. Gallen station restaurant, over lunch, while he's dissecting the sole: "What is a murderer, really? Can you tell me?" He looks at me insistently. I: "No, the line is far too hazy!" He, after a long pause: "Isn't a successful writer also a murderer, in his own way?" Later we come to speak of Dostoevsky's Rodion Raskolnikov, who, under psychic pressure, kills an antiques dealer. We both consider this book one of the most disturbing crime novels in world literature. Robert says that Dostoevsky could never have written it without his experiences facing the firing squad and in Siberia. "Thus pain often has a purpose after all. Usually we simply don't see it."

Robert has much to say on the topic of updating literature for a contemporary audience. I tell him that a rather disrespectful adaption of Shakespeare's *The Tempest* by the film director Erich Engel was recently put on at the Zürich Schauspielhaus. Robert replies: "Shakespeare and Schlegel don't need us to pretend to like them. Anyone who doesn't have time to see Shakespeare unabridged should stay home and read Vicki Baum. I have seen abridged versions of works by Jean Paul and Jeremias Gotthelf. They were unbearable. For it is precisely the longueurs and twists, the superfluous width and height that make them beautiful. Knowing that the truncated version of Kleist's *Penthesilea* mounted only once in Berlin by one Jakob Walser was a miserable flop still makes me happy."

Robert speaks in monosyllables of the Christmas celebration

at the asylum: "It might have been nice for children. We elderly are too old for it." His need to distance himself is particularly noticeable today. This morning he has already led me like a tramp off the well-traveled tracks and onto slippery, marshy and half-frozen woodland paths. My feeble objections—that I was ravenous, since I had gotten up at five thirty in the morning, that I had no breakfast in my belly, and that my military shoes were apparently not stout enough, since I was running around with wet, ice-cold feet—made no impression on him. He tells me *en passant* that the only few thousand marcs he'd ever had—partly from the prize he'd been awarded by the Society of Rhenish Women at Wilhelm Schäfer's recommendation, and partly saved from honoraria—had been lost through inflation. Since then he had only ever lived in poverty. Back then the women's society had also invited him to Leipzig to sign a few hundred books. Afterwards he had gone to visit his ailing brother Karl in Berlin.

The sun is shining when we tear ourselves away from the station restaurant's Christmas menu, which we washed down with Dôle de Sion. We climb the hill opposite the Rosenberg, which looks out between firs and alders onto the snow-blanketed Säntis mountain chain, and to Vögelinsegg. We enjoy these springlike hours, praising the woods, Lake Constance, which shimmers like a landscape of dunes, and the joy of walking. Robert is now much wearier than I, slipping often on the steep wooded ground, and he suggests taking the train to Herisau from Haggen. We stand around at the station for a while, and I urge him to go home, for perhaps a second good Christmas meal awaits him there.

He goes, but reluctantly. I watch him for a long time as he walks home; with his rounded back he looks like a weary Sherpa.

On the train from Gossau to Winterthur my heart almost stops. Somewhere along the way I lost my notebook, which contains the beginnings of many poems, and even some finished ones, including one whose ending just occurred to me this morning, after many months of waiting. It begins thus: "Loveliness pains. But so does/ Beauty's slight. Pain: the breath of/ The wind that from distant mountains blows …!"

February 1953

DURING OUR MOST recent walk Robert remarked that the trial of Anna Koch would have made a good subject for Kleist or Dostoevsky: "But one must stick to the truth, which is often more fantastic than a writer's imagination."

"I will do it," I promised, "and I'll send you the result before our next walk." Here it is:

Above the town of Gonten in Appenzell rises the Hüttenberg. There Anna Koch was born, daughter of a poor peasant farmer, on August 23, 1831. She had eleven siblings, seven of whom died in childhood. In order to feed the large family, her father took on embroidery work. Anna grew into a splendid, proud blonde, who took up with men at quite a young age. She decked herself out with jewelry that she bought on installment. It is said that her foolish mother only encouraged her, and did not remind her of her religious duties. Her father, a good, quiet man, died of a stroke shortly after his daughter's beheading.

On June 8, 1849, the Feast of Corpus Christi, Anna watched the traditional procession in Gonten. On her way home for the midday meal, she met Johann Baptist Mazenauer, who was four years her elder, and worked in the parish as a mason. She started in on him immediately, accusing him of having taken up with her childhood friend Magdalena Fässler, who, like Anna, came from a large peasant family, but unlike her, had a reputation for being a virtuous girl. For his part, the awkward, stolid Mazenauer, who was known in the area as a decent if physically unimpressive fellow, told Anna he'd heard that she was running around Appenzell with strangers. It was hardly her place, therefore, to be making accusations. Then he tried to reassure her and they went their separate ways.

The usual vespers were held that afternoon in Gonten. Since a big storm was brewing, the flock of churchgoers was smaller than normal. Anna was not among them. In fact, shortly before the beginning of vespers she had met Magdalena Fässler in the churchyard. Anna told Magdalena that she had lost her rosary along the way, and asked for help finding it. Her friend agreed, as long as it wouldn't cause her to miss vespers. As they were walking together, Anna pushed the sweet-natured Magdalena into the so-called Teichelrose out of jealousy. This Teichelrose is a small pond surrounded by woods; the approaching storm meant they would be unlikely to encounter any passersby. Anna held Magdalena's head under water until she gave no sign of life. Two days later she sold a few pieces of her victim's jewelry, including a silver necklace, in Appenzell.

When Magdalena failed to arrive home that evening, a search was mounted in Gonten. The villagers, however, singing and dancing in the taverns, started the rumor that her disappearance was easily explained by the fact that her stepmother was a nasty shrew. People assumed, therefore, that Magdalena had run away to her relatives on account of some quarrel. It was only four days later that a farmer reported having seen Magdalena floating on her back in the Teichelrose. The corpse was thereupon carried to her parents' house on a bier, where many people had gathered to pray for the salvation of her soul. At her mother's urging, Anna also went to the Fässler house, where she nonetheless refused to sprinkle the dead girl with holy water. While genuflecting, she fainted, which caused something of a sensation. On the way home Anna's mother begged her daughter to keep quiet if she had done something wrong, for it could cost her her head.

Despite her silence, Anna was called to the town hall for questioning on June 14, along with Baptist Mazenauer, who was known to the villagers as "Bisch." Between then and November 26 a long series of hearings was conducted by an examining judge, the governor, and the head of the cantonal assembly, and the possibility that Magdalena's death could have been an accident was scrupulously considered. There were twenty-nine hearings altogether, during which Anna and Bisch were repeatedly accused and raked over the coals. At first, the pretty Anna Koch was given preferential treatment, being allowed to stay with the town bailiff's family and receive visitors during the day, while Bisch was kept in jail from the beginning, where he had to sleep on half-rotten straw. Although he stubbornly protested his innocence, maintaining that he was as innocent as Christ on the cross, no one believed him. During his twenty-three weeks of imprisonment—including seven weeks on bread and water—he received 150 blows of the rod on his back and buttocks. Furthermore he was subjected to thumbscrews and put in the "Bocksfutter," wherein his hands were bound together under his knees, with wooden stakes between his knees and arms, so that he could neither sit nor stand. Bisch was forced to remain in this position for an hour and a quarter. At first Anna tried to exonerate her friend by claiming that he had found the murdered girl's jewelry while walking home and had given it to her with the promise that they would be married in the fall. Later she practically accused him of murdering Magdalena. Since she became more and more tangled in her own lies, she was also occasionally flogged by the Appenzell night watchman or the executioner, who had been summoned on September 6 from Altstätten. Once, the day before the annual fair was to be held in Gonten, Anna ran away from the town hall, roamed about for a long time, and tried to unburden her tortured soul in a pilgrimage church. She also toyed with the idea of taking her own life, but couldn't summon the courage. The next evening, after a secret visit to her parents' house, she returned voluntarily to the town hall. Only on October 27, at the twentieth hearing—after declaring that she was pregnant by Bisch—did she make a first partial confession. On November 17, after relapses in which she accused both her supposed bridegroom and her mother of complicity, she admitted that Bisch was completely innocent. Nonetheless, he was not released until November 28, at which point he was so emaciated and feeble that he could barely stand. Still, he magnanimously forgave Anna her lies. Later when he requested compensation from the court for the agonies he had endured despite his innocence, he was denied on the grounds that he had been obdurate and had acted foolishly during the hearings. The only thing that he was granted was an official declaration stating that he had been wrongfully imprisoned. "Poor fool," as Baptist Mazenauer called himself, used this to ask for alms from kindhearted people by selling leaflets printed with the sermon given after Anna's beheading. Though he traipsed all the way to St. Gallen, the leaflets barely earned him a hundred francs. In 1853 he married a girl of low birth and fashioned a tiny cottage out of a former goat pen where the couple lived, destitute but content. When in 1870 the canton of Inner Rhodes advertised for a new bailiff, "Bisch" applied for the position with the following words: "I am a poor, infirm man with three small illkempt children, because twenty years ago I innocently suffered a lot and thereafter was practically unfit for work. Asking you all therefore for heavensake for pity and mercy. I want to promise you, if you entrust me with this office, to earn the greatest satisfaction of the people in all my authority with sweat, obedience, and discretion. I commend myself to your benevolence and goodness." The post, however, was given to one of his nine competitors. "Bisch" died in early May 1902 at the age of seventy-five.

On November 29, 1849, a special committee of the cantonal assembly handed down the verdict that the murderess was to be beheaded. This was conveyed to Anna Koch by a capuchin friar. She sank to the ground, unconscious from the shock. The next day she was given the last rites. On December 3, the Great Council confirmed the death sentence. To hear the final verdict, Anna was made to walk up the stone steps from the town hall to the street, which was filled with curious onlookers. At the town hall, the head of the cantonal assembly of Appenzell Inner Rhodes read out the text of the verdict, which was to be carried out immediately. When the murderess once again fainted, her temples were rubbed with freshly fallen snow. According to J. E. Neff's stylistically clumsy account, when she awoke, the executioner and his assistant tried to lift her onto the sleigh for the condemned. But Anna, once again full of lust for life, batted the men away like flies. Only the crucifix, which the friar held up with the words: "Look on this—this innocent one suffered death. But you are guilty!" seemed to give her some peace. She now voluntarily mounted the sleigh with the friar and the pastor of Appenzell, and the three rode through the snowy village to the site of the execution. People were gathered everywhere, shamelessly gaping at the unfortunate girl from roofs, windows, and streets, as nearly always happens in such circumstances. Anna let out occasional bloodcurdling cries between the comforting words of the two clergymen, wildly shaking her loose hair in her terror of death.

At the sight of the scaffold she moaned so terribly that people feared she had taken leave of her senses. Anna had to be carried up the three steps to the block in a state of semiconsciousness. When she opened her eyes, she kissed the crucifix that was held close to her face and allowed the black hood to be placed over her eyes without protest. But she pressed her shoulders so firmly against her head that the executioner could find no spot upon which to exercise his duty. Perhaps the condemned girl knew that according to unwritten law, no execution could be carried out after sundown. In this state of impasse, a spectator from Mettlen called out: "Hen der no nie gseh, wie d'Rhintaler d'Herdefel wegid?" which means something like: "Haven't you seen how they weigh potatoes in the Rhine Valley?" Now a roof lath was fetched from nearby, to which the delinquent's hair was bound. Two men took hold of the board, one on each side, and pulled upward, so that Anna's neck began to stretch and the double-edged sword could finally whoosh down upon it.

In full sight of the corpse that now lay on the scaffold, one of the two clergymen gave the traditional sermon, in which he pointed out the tragic consequences of increasing godlessness and moral corruption. After the speech the executioner's assistant placed the head and body into a prepared casket, which was driven to the cemetery of the condemned and lowered into the grave with only a few people in attendance.

The grave was soon covered with fresh snow.

April 12, 1953

THREE DAYS BEFORE Robert's seventy-fifth birthday. The doctor told me on the telephone that a lengthy article about Robert had been published in the Appenzell newspaper, in which I was mentioned as his guardian and only friend. For this reason, I look forward to our meeting today with somewhat mixed feelings. Won't he be even more suspicious than usual?

But no, he greets me under the forget-me-not-blue sky unusually cheerfully and immediately agrees to spend today gypsying around Herisau. Up hills and down. In the gardens, the golden yellow of forsythia, daffodils, and primroses. The fruit trees a vestal green. And over everything the forget-me-not-blue canopy of the sky.

I tell Robert about *Katie of Heilbronn*, which I saw at the theater and found very disappointing. Robert: "I can imagine. For me the character is too much like a faithful puppy. She's always fawning around Count von Strahl. In fact I prefer the noblewoman Kunigunde. She scratches and bites, which men like. Admittedly, when these snooty types grow vulgar it can be almost intolerable. Heinrich von Kleist was clearly rebuffed by one such and the shrewish character of Kunigunde was his revenge. Self-indulgent, as indeed he was. Kleist, by the way, is a curious writer: when he means to be lyrical he turns dramatic, and when he tries to write plays he turns lyrical, as in *Katie of Heilbronn*. It has been a good quarter century since I've read the play. But I still remember the line: 'Murder creeps about in socks.' Something like that, isn't it? How often in my life have I run into Kleist! In Thun and by Lake Constance, where he and Henriette Vogel took their own lives, and where I stood before their graves. And then in Berlin, when Kaiser Wilhelm II quoted a line from *The Prince of Homburg* from the balcony of his castle at the outbreak of the First World War. To incite his subjects against the French, of course."

The Dane J. P. Jacobsen gives us our second literary subject of the birthday celebration. Before lunch in Herisau, which we take in a little inn accompanied by cloudy cider, Robert tells me the story of "Mrs. Fonss," which was published seventy years ago. The story concerns the noble character of a wealthy forty-year-old widow who lives with her two children in the Danish provinces. One day a lover from her youth appears, having sold his sheep farm in the South American pampas. He immediately falls back in love with his former sweetheart, whom circumstances prevented him from marrying twenty years ago. Now Mrs. Fonss too wishes to claim her right to happiness. They are married within a few days. Since the children cry and rage that their mother is being unfaithful to their father and them, the couple move to Spain, where they are happy for a few years, in spite of the grief the mother suffers at being estranged from her children. Then Mrs. Fonss falls fatally ill and writes her children an affectionate farewell letter wherein she begs them to consider after her death the fact that she was never so loved as by him who will hold her hand at the end ... Robert remembers many details of this melancholy tale.

In the afternoon, a long conversation about Stalin's mysterious death. "I was repulsed by the stink of incense that was always wafting about him," Robert says. "Surrounded by slavish followers, he ultimately turned into an idol who could no longer live like a normal person. Perhaps there were some traces of genius in him. But a nation is better ruled by a mediocre character. Wickedness nearly always lurks in genius, wickedness that the people pay for in pain, blood, and disgrace."

On the day of his seventy-fifth birthday, Robert was rather grumpy after a report from Dr. Steiner. If anyone mentioned the tributes he received that day in the newspapers and on the radio, he would answer: "That's nothing to me!" As on every other workday, he did his chores conscientiously, sweeping the floor of the sitting room, and folding paper bags in the afternoon.

During his birthday it began to snow gently. When Dr. Steiner's wife told her children how beautifully Robert Walser had written about snow, winter, and the cold, they said that it must be snowing because it was Herr Walser's birthday today, and he liked winter so much.

August 30, 1953

FOR THE FIRST time Robert gives me the impression of an aging man struggling against his physical decline. The blazing sun makes today's walk particularly strenuous. At first our plan was to swim in Lake Constance. But in Rorschach, Robert suddenly takes off in a different direction, toward woods redolent of mushrooms and fir trees. Then across fields. Up hills, down hills, wading once through a deep stream. Robert often stops at the edge of the woods, his hand cupped around his ear, his head bent toward the ground, sniffing about. I'm reminded of the distant days of my youth, playing cowboys and Indians. Sometimes Robert talks to himself, rails at the rude motorists, skittering away from them in outrage whenever we cross a road, and swinging far wide of yapping farmyard dogs. But what strikes me about him most today is his labored, sluggish gait and the frequency with which he lags behind me, particularly on the steaming asphalt roads, where he looks, with the expired cigarette in his mouth and 'high-water pants,' like a work-ravaged farmer. He wears a gray felt hat, which he pushes aside brusquely from time to time. His forehead has grown bright red in the noon sun.

It's a beautiful, bright-blue day with golden-green meadows and fawn-colored cows, the gardens brilliant with zinnias, geraniums, and gladiolas; there are already autumn crocuses with their old-maidenly violet petals. Apples, plums, and cider pears crowd the trees in blessed abundance. The wet summer has been followed by a fruit-rich autumn.

We are less lucky with our meal. Our *café complet* is served by a pretty, fiery-cheeked girl, who is however in a terrible mood. Above us hangs a crucifix. From the adjacent kitchen we hear minutes on end of scolding and screeching between quarreling women and children, while the pretty waitress's voice rises above them all. Afterward it grows quieter. Only the pans and dishes rattle, as if continuing the quarrel. Then we hear a murmured litany from the kitchen. It is the family, saying their morning prayers.

On the way Robert asks me whether I have written any plays. I answer: "The adaptation of Nestroy's farce *The Torn One* that I did with Alfred Polgar, which has been produced about two dozen times at the Zürich Schauspielhaus, is my only sin in this domain. And you? Have you tried it?" Robert replies: "Yes, but nothing really came of it. Drama requires a more crooked character. Think of Schiller!" He talks of the poet Max Dauthendey, with whom he once spent a wonderful week in Würzburg. Dauthendey's father was the first portrait photographer in Russia. Robert also had some good times with Wedekind in Munich. A stimulating, but uncanny person, full of demonic pitfalls. Robert didn't want to see him on stage: "Poets usually take themselves far too seriously as actors. The actor's art is overrated these days in general. The crucial thing is what the writer says and how he says it. This whole song and dance about Max Reinhardt & Co. has something indiscrete and narcissistic about it. For my part, I've been amused even by third-rate stagings and actors. The most sophisticated thing is definitely not always the most digestible." We talk for a long time of Sophocles' *Oedipus Rex* and Hölderlin's adaptation of it. Robert is enraptured by the play, and finds the sexual relationship between mother and son not unequivocally abhorrent. Something beautiful could also come of it—Antigone, for example. But of course incest must be forbidden for social reasons. This is the younger generation's safeguard against the older one's lust for preservation and possession. I tell him what curious customs have been preserved among Orthodox Jews. At his request I describe my visit to the house of prayer of an Orthodox sect in Zürich-Aussersihl on a Saturday evening. My companion was the Yiddish poet Lajzar Ajchenrand, who lived in Zürich as an emigrant at the time. He had grown up near the Polish county seat of Lublin as the son of a small-town tailor, a profession that he also follows. Once his father came home utterly distraught because anti-Semites had cut off his beard. For weeks he didn't dare to leave the house, as it was the most scandalous dishonor that could have been done to him. Anyway, on that Sabbath evening Ajchenrand and I arrived somewhat late at the synagogue, where the wearing of hats is required. The ritual prayers and songs, which begin at dusk, were already nearing their end. But still some of the more devout were in ecstatic trances, chanting and waving their arms vigorously, eyes burning. In the same room, another group was already talking merrily of business and family affairs. When we entered the synagogue two pale boys had shaken our hands with a polite "Shalom!" Like the other entrants, we fished out some herring from a metal dish where several pieces swam in vinegar water. Then we approached a group of men who were sitting, chatting at a wooden table, pouring themselves beer to go with their bread. In the next room the women and girls were also celebrating the Sabbath. As the last worshippers prepared to go home, a slim man of about forty began telling his tale of woe. In Yiddish he reported that he was originally from Kiev, and was an upholsterer by trade. He had fought in Israel against the English and the Arabs. Later he had been recruited by a Jewish organization to smuggle Jews out of Hungary and Czechoslovakia to Israel. Twice he had been caught, and had avoided harsh punishment only by escaping. The identity papers that he waved around were indeed covered with countless stamps and notations in foreign languages. His interlocutor was a short rabbi, a little white-haired man with a rosy complexion fresh as a piglet's. While the stranger, who wanted to travel via Switzerland to a kibbutz in Israel, moaned and gesticulated dramatically, the rabbi smiled archly, but not unkindly. One could see that he was used to such scenes. His bright eyes stood in glaring contrast to the despairing looks that the stranger shot at the little group who listened to the dispute, half-curious, half-bored or wary in case the scene should devolve into begging. The stranger accused the Jews of Zürich of having hearts of stone: "No one wants to help—everyone helps only himself!" The rabbi reminded him that tomorrow was a new day. Surely he would find a solution. No Jew had ever starved to death in Zürich. At these words his gentle voice rose to a forte, for according to a Yiddish saying, one can only silence a raging dog with louder barking. And indeed: everyone seemed tired of speaking, and turned toward the dark street.

As did the poet and I. We went to a Jewish restaurant to eat cold carp. It was not particularly cozy there—a faceless place with faceless people. You could smell the pedantic cleanliness of Zürich. I would have preferred an authentic taste of the eastern Jewry. But I did hear all kinds of interesting things about Orthodox customs, at which Western European Jews often unfairly turn up their noses. I was told that during Pesach-Haggadah, which commemorates the exodus of the people of Israel from Egypt, the head of the family lies comfortably stretched out, half-prone, in a chair, to symbolize the freedom of the Jews after their prolonged enslavement. The family clusters around the patriarch, who tells the story of the exodus. Full of curiosity, the children ask him questions, and perhaps someone will toss in the following joke: A goy asks why the Jews don't work with their hands. Answer: "Because they still hurt from making bricks in Egypt!" Curious too is the chivalric custom of many Chassidim, that in the night between Friday and Saturday—during the Sabbath, that is—a husband is supposed to sleep with his wife. First he throws his skullcap into his wife's bed. If she does not throw it back, but rather keeps it in bed, he knows that he is welcome. In the opposite case, he must forego the congress. Should he disregard this age-old custom, a rabbi can pronounce them divorced at the woman's request. "The old lawgivers were no fools," Robert said. "Their aims are, however, often interpreted far too rationalistically these days."

December 27, 1953

MORNING SNACK AT the Rorschach station restaurant. A half-drunken man is running his yap like a mill wheel. Robert sits as if glued to his seat. I suggest we walk along the light-gray lake to Arbon. He parries the idea, however, and chooses the opposite direction, only to finally pivot 180 degrees and aim for St. Gallen. The upshot: a quarter of an hour later, chatting gaily, we're climbing near the "five-country vista." The valley lies green at our feet. But the farther we walk, the deeper we find ourselves in newly fallen snow; Robert, despite the biting wind, without an overcoat or warm underthings, I in light shoes. Gradually the area around Lake Constance darkens. We lose our sense of direction, having wandered quite a while in the woods, without, by the way, meeting a single person. Finally we're on a ridge, huffing and puffing our way forward. After half an hour I knock at a farmhouse to ask the way. A large family is sitting in the living room; a homey Christmas tree stands behind the table. The young farmer comes to the door and tells us we are in the vicinity of Eggersriet. It is now nearly noon. We turn steeply up toward St. Gallen. Robert grows monosyllabic, clearly fighting exhaustion. At the edge of St. Gallen I tell him that Heinrich Simon, the former owner of the *Frankfurter Zeitung*, was murdered in New York by a homosexual. That interests him. He tells me that Simon had bought a painting his brother Karl made from a photograph of him—Robert—sitting dreamily on a boulder near a birch tree at the edge of the woods. Did I remember it? It had been reproduced in the magazine *Der Lesezirkel*. "Yes, I remember the picture, but your brother Oscar's wife Fridolina told me that according to your sister Lisa, you destroyed it!" "That may be," Robert says, cloaking himself in silence once more.

Now we take the tram to the St. Gallen train station, whose restaurant we enter with such stiff paws that at first we can hardly hold our soup spoons. We then delight in the menu for a long time, and since Robert seems comfortable, I risk asking him why his novel *Theodor*, which he read from in March 1922 in Zürich, was never published. To my astonishment he answers affably: "After I finished the manuscript I sent it to Verlag Grethlein, but they didn't want to publish it. Where it ended up later I don't know." "Max Rychner published two episodes from the novel," I recall, "in 1923 in *Wissen und Leben*, the magazine he edited, among them the excerpt in which Theodor describes coming to a Berlin art salon in search of a job." But Robert waves this off: *"Assez de ces temps passés!"*

Good Friday 1954

SNOW IS FALLING when I set out for the train station at five o'clock in the morning. It looks like bits of paper from another world: cheerless flakes—some small, some chunky—swirling haphazardly around each other. It's a peculiar snow—ominous, as if it's trying to murmur: "Here I am—I, the snow from another world!"

On the ride to eastern Switzerland the houses, garden fences, and fields all lie buried under winter's polar bear coat. Few people are on the train, most of them dozing dully with their little packages. I have the impression that day hardly dares to dawn. In Zürich I heard birds twittering in the dawn light, but here in this apocalyptic atmosphere their song sounds to me more like a funeral dirge.

At the station: Robert with his umbrella, but without a coat—I with a coat, but without an umbrella. It's snowing heavily. He climbs into my compartment, lights a cheroot, and asks cheerily, "How're you?" Most of the skiers disembark with their skis in Urnäsch. Now we are practically the only passengers until Appenzell. We set off immediately through the silent village on the path to Gais. At least two dozen jackdaws are circling the castle screeching. Shortly after we cross the bridge over the Sitter, we meet a funeral procession. A weary, black-shrouded horse pulls the hearse, which is topped with three wreaths. Then follows a long double column of mourners, their open umbrellas forming a kind of tunnel, from which curious faces, wrinkled and murmuring litanies, peer out at us. Most are the faces of old, worn-out women. Many have bright-red cheeks. Later I asked a waitress if she knew who had died. "A real old 'un, who lost 'er mind!"

The snow has now turned to hail. Sharp bits of ice fly in our faces. But we march on toward Gais. We can no longer hear the litany. Instead, we hear the squealing of hungry pigs. Suddenly Robert stops and says: "This really is ghastly weather—let's turn back!" No sooner said than done. We take the same way back and see to our astonishment that the cortege has gotten no further than the Sitter bridge. As if they were waiting for us. We hear the murmuring again, which upsets Robert. He does not like to think of death. He tugs at my sleeve, as if the dirge is chasing him: "Let us go to Gais after all!" We plod about a hundred meters forward again through the slush. But the grains of ice bite into our faces even more fiercely than before. Bit by bit the world has transformed into a brown sauce. A car splashes it all over us. Again we retreat, at Robert's request, but this time into a snug tavern, where we breakfast lavishly. He brusquely rejects my proposal to wander around the castle, which contains an historical collection: "No, no, we must aim steadfastly for Gais, where I once spent a happy time with my sister Lisa." Snow flurries there too. But the village square almost seems to cast a spell over Robert. He stops reverently and breathes deep of the homey atmosphere, calling my attention to the church, the sweep of the gable, the grandness and personality of each house. "Like something from a dream!" he breathes. I photograph him like this, hastily and nervously, just to have another picture of him, a memento for later. In the Krone we carve up a rather dry pike, which we wash down with Beaujolais, then follow with meringues. Our striking waitress arrogantly keeps her distance; she's clearly saving herself for better customers—motoring guests. Over black coffee Robert points out Byron's striking similarity to Raphael. Both matured early and died early. He lists all of Byron's works and describes his adventure-filled life and his feverish end in the swamp town of Missolonghi, amid the Greek rebels, who revered him like a prince. And he remembers the pain Goethe felt in Weimar at the news of the death of this "incommensurable talent."

Afterward I ask Robert if he ever met Carl Spitteler in person, for when remembering the philhellene creator of "Manfred" and "The Prisoner of Chillon," one might also pay homage to the author of "Olympian Spring" ... but his reaction is rather cool: "No, I never spoke to him. But my publisher Cassirer once sent him one of my novels, which resulted in a very snide letter I received from Spitteler." Personally, Robert had derived fleeting enjoyment from *Conrad the Lieutenant*. This prose work by Spitteler led us to exchange our own military experiences. Robert tells me that he did basic training in Bern before his seven-year stay in Berlin. There he was usually posted to border or drill duty. He had never been in the first call-up. After his return to Switzerland he was immediately transferred to the militia.

September 30, 1954

ON OUR LEISURELY walk through meadows and woods to St. Gallen I tell Robert of my trip to Venice, and of the detour I made with Max Picard to the lagoon island of Torcello, whose cathedral contains a Romanesque pillared basilica and early medieval mosaics. Associations flock to Robert from every direction like butterflies: Shakespeare's *The Merchant of Venice*, Goldoni, Casanova, Stendhal, Richard Wagner. A long debate about sons of famous fathers, who, according to Robert, are best off shipped to boarding school: "There they can develop into themselves, far away from their fathers' hangers-on and untouched by the hunger for fame ... Personally, not even the most famous father could have gotten to me. Calmly and modestly going one's own way is the surest path to happiness." He tells me that a certain Herr Pushkin has been posted to Berlin as a Soviet diplomat. He looks fat and cruel, like a spiteful caricature by Pushkin the poet, whom even Lenin, the uncultured Bolshevist chief, had to respect.

I tell him jokingly that now he has to respect me a little bit too, as the Zürich city council voted me onto the committee for literature. He doubles over with laughter, which infects me too: "Aha, so that's why you look so city-councilly and Röbeli Faesi-like! You're really climbing the ladder!"

We climb over electric fences and end up in a deep ravine, where Robert calls out: "Up out of Hades! How far we've strayed!" As we're climbing out he often shakes his head dubiously. I remark with some concern that he seems to have lost a great deal of weight. But he parries fiercely: "Stop that! Let's not talk about my health." Finally we reach the summit of the "Solitüde," an 872-meter high hill with a nice view over St. Gallen. Longingly I fix my eagle eye on an inn a little way down below, but Robert won't hear of it. We hike onward to St. Gallen. He tells me that in 1895 and 1896, when he was working in Stuttgart for the Deutsche Verlagsgesellschaft and for Cotta, he often visited the Rococo pleasure palace "Solitüde," which once housed the Karlsschule, the military academy made famous by Schiller's attendance.

Once Robert lived as a freelance writer for a few weeks in Munich, and went to Oktoberfest with Alfred Kubin. He had been introduced to Kubin by the urbane Franz Blei.

Christmas 1954

THE FEELING OF being shut out, the loneliness of those who live outside the circle of family, is never so strong as at Christmas. During our morning walk we're speaking of the ethical value of building a family, when Robert pokes me in the ribs and points at two passing women: "Didn't you notice how scornfully they looked at us? As if we were riffraff ...?" "Or pietists brooding," I add, and Robert laughs: "Yes, for women we're damaged goods. We have to come to terms with that, for better or worse."

From Herisau we've turned toward the ruins of a castle, high up on a peak. As if on command, it had begun to snow as soon as I got off the train. My right foot hurts because of a pulled tendon, but I don't want to spoil Robert's pleasure in our Christmas walk. A beautiful collie darts toward us over the quiet snowy field, legs flying, then jumps up as if he's been waiting for us a long time. Robert tries to push him away: "Geh 'way, ye silly beast!" But the dog's devotion is undimmed. He sniffs forward a bit, then returns to us, and after a few minutes Robert has gotten used to him. When I tell him how classy he looks today, in a new gray jacket and new shoes, he's silent. Then we speak for a long time of Heinrich von Kleist. I tell him of a lecture where Thomas Mann put forth the thesis that the first act of Kleist's unfinished tragedy *Robert Guiskard* was so successful that Kleist couldn't outdo it. Robert considers this view false: *Guiskard* is not a good piece; from the beginning Kleist had spent himself too early, it was obvious that the breakdown was inevitable. Goethe was right to disapprove of this young comet. The harmonious world had a legitimate right to push away anything discordant.

When Robert questions me about my Christmas experiences, I tell him that I once rowed with a British missionary to the South Sea island of Malakula, whose inhabitants were said to be real live cannibals. As we approached the interior, several wild-looking, armed men with pieces of bamboo stuck through their broad noses emerged from the bush. They were naked apart from some leaves covering their loins. Their expressions were rather fierce, not Christmas-like at all. But the missionary had the funny idea to remove his false teeth, which so stunned the superstitious islanders that they stared dumbfounded at my companion and made signs to suggest they had no malicious intentions. In any case they decided not to make us their holiday roast. "In fact the so-called bad people are often not nearly as bad as the so-called good people. A few days ago," I continue, "I celebrated Christmas in the Zürich prison of Regensdorf. During dinner with the director and some official guests I learned the following: In the year 1914, the prison director told the inmates after Sunday services that there was a plan to start a prison choir. Anyone who was interested should apply to the conductor, Ernst Honegger. The latter undertook to test the applicants' voices and ears. He then presented the ten best singers to the prison director, who looked horrified, took Honegger aside, and said 'How strange! You want to form a choir of ten murderers, of all things!'" Robert: "That couldn't have been a coincidence. Most murders are crimes of passion. And don't most artists have passionate natures? And are singers not artists?"

After this observation I continue: "The conductor confessed to me that he was often sorry to lose his most gifted singers when their sentences were up. Once he had a powerful bass who could have sung with the Don Cossack Choir. Another inmate, who had murdered his mother and had been his best lyric tenor, made a career as a musician in Rome after his release." Robert: "It could be a novella, or even an opera: a jail conductor is so enamored of a voice that he incites its owner to commit a crime so that he can sing in the choir. By the way, such gifts are often passed down through the generations. In my family I am not the only one who wrote verse. My brothers Ernst and Hermann were also infected with the poetic fever; my sister-in-law Fridolina as well. So you see: such romantic notions can spread like an epidemic. In the time of the brothers Schlegel, Tieck, and Novalis, there were often many artistic flowers on the same family tree—women as well as men."

Good Friday 1955

IN MARCH I hear disquieting reports about Robert. He had to be brought to the hospital for a flu-like inflammation of the lungs. High fever and bloody phlegm; fever rapidly reduced with penicillin, then slight relapses of elevated temperature. The doctors recommend that I walk with him only around the grounds of the asylum.

How astonished I am, therefore, to see Robert standing at the train station in a black overcoat! He laughingly agrees, however, to take a more leisurely pace than usual. Slowly we climb toward the woods and the ruin that we visited last time. He is particularly fond of this route. He breathes heavily as we ascend, but nonetheless lights two cigarettes during the three-hour walk, contrary to his custom. When I remark that I was recently invited to Warsaw, Moscow, Irkutsk, and Peking, we discover that Dostoevsky's *House of the Dead* is one of our mutual favorites. With evident emotion Robert remembers the episode in which the otherwise brutish convicts take pity on the lame-winged steppe eagle which lived with them for three months, throwing it from the rampart and watching with longing as it hops away across the autumnal steppe …

Then Robert tells me that he has been reading with great pleasure *In the Corner Window*, a four-volume novel about an officer, written by the Hamburg seaman and hotelier Friedrich Gerstäcker, as well as Jules Verne's *In Search of the Castaways*. At my news that a young English poet, Christopher Middleton, who teaches literature at a university in London, has translated into English his "The Walk" and "Kleist in Thun" with admirable sensitivity, he answers with a curt "Really!"

Before I depart I visit Dr. Steiner, who says he advised Robert not to leave the grounds of the asylum. Robert insisted, however, on picking me up at the station. Since his heart is in serious condition, any greater exertion will put him at risk of a heart attack. I ask whether during his indisposition Robert had been more trusting of the nurses than he was of the regular staff and patients; the doctor says no, mostly he turned to the wall and wouldn't take even fruit juice to quench his thirst. According to him, water was sufficient.

July 17, 1955

SWISS FEDERAL GYMNASTICS Festival in Zürich. It seems as if the whole city is tipsy. Young men saunter barefoot down the main street yodeling, jostling women, and making lewd jokes. Only alcohol seems to unlock the Swiss gift for clownery and childish masquerades. The joy they take in shabby carnival kitsch and all sorts of tasteless things is depressing: little Tyrolean hats, plush dolls, miniature beer steins and the like; it is no consolation that this lack of stylistic sense has become an international epidemic.

A bluish-white sky over the verdant, rain-fed landscape; scraps of fog float down now and then between Zürich and Wil. The train half-empty. In Gossau Robert asks me rather brusquely where we're off to. I answer: "To St. Margrethen!" He grows silent, and broods during the ride over what I might have in store for him. Finally he asks: "Shall we breakfast there?" Yes, of course, I am hungry too. During our breakfast at the station restaurant the conversation flows rather like resin. Then we climb steeply upward through the woods toward Walzenhausen, stopping by romantic streams, and begin to talk of Tolstoy's *Resurrection*. We agree that this late work, which the author wrote at the end of the last century, laboring under the guilt of a sin from his youth—as a young officer he had seduced one of his aunt's servants and left her destitute—is one of humanity's most sacred books. I remind Robert of the wonderful scene where Prince Nekhlyudov brings Maslova the news that the court has refused to pardon her as she's waiting to be taken to Siberia. He is very agitated. But when the warden tells him that Maslova has been sent from the hospital back to prison for engaging in intimate relations with a doctor, his feelings cool. He greets her icily, and she blushes, for she guesses the reason for his ill humor (only later does the prince discover that she put up fierce resistance to the doctor's attempted rape, and is completely innocent in the affair). The prince's battle against his own demons is one in a series of keen psychological insights in the novel. Robert also remembers the schnapps-drinking worker on the train that takes the prince to Siberia, who says to him and the other third-class passengers in response to their disapproving looks: "Of course, everyone looks when I drink, but no one looks when I work." Perhaps to irritate me, Robert makes a snide comment about prostitutes, of whom Maslova was one, by approving of the severity of the English, who recently hanged a bargirl for shooting her unfaithful lover. Society must scrupulously demand of women the conservative family spirit. I say that Tolstoy never judged as harshly as he. For it is the former bordello girl Maslova who makes the greatest sacrifice in the name of human love by marrying the unloved Vladimir Ivanovich and giving the prince his freedom. So we argue back and forth over this and Tolstoy's citation of Thoreau, that every honest citizen of a state that still allows slavery should be in jail.

Gradually however, the heat of the dog day begins to get to Robert. He walks ever slower, locked in silence. Then suddenly he stops and nearly collapses. He growls that he has bad cramps in both his legs. He refuses, however, to sit or lie down. Angrily he flails about as if fending off an invisible enemy, tries a few knee bends, and makes clumsy starts to the right and the left. I dare not help him. Near Wolfhalden the cramps return with such severity that he suggests turning toward a train or bus station as soon as we can. I ask an older woman, who peeks out of a weaving studio, about the closest train or bus station, implying that my companion is having trouble walking. Robert murmurs a colorful curse as the woman points out the path to Rheineck. As we climb slowly, he says conciliatorily: "It is indeed sometimes quite a good idea to be friendly to people!"

Lunch at Ochsen in Rheineck. The beer makes us both sleepy. We doze until the train leaves, and then in the compartment. Is his condition more serious than I realize? I am wracked with worry. As we part his last words are: "Did you see the heavenly colors of Lake Constance?"

Christmas 1955

A RAIN-DREARY MORNING, which at midday shows more inclination toward night than day. Only a few travelers, as the pre-spring green of the meadows and woods do not encourage winter sports. On the way to St. Gallen we engage in a meticulous discussion of Kleist, whose *Broken Jug* I saw a few days ago at the Schauspielhaus. I describe the bet with Zschokke and

Wieland in Bern that had led to the composition of this comedy, Goethe's dismissive judgment, and the botched premiere in Weimar, where people whistled and jeered. Robert remembers seeing *The Prince of Homburg* in Stuttgart when he was an apprentice in the book trade. Recently he read Adalbert Stifter's *Witiko*, which he found "exasperatingly boring." Stifter's creative powers must already have been greatly reduced at that point.

He speaks disparagingly of the now-commonplace practice of lavishing writing prizes on mere beginners: "When one spoils them from the very start, they remain schoolboys forever. To become a man takes suffering, underappreciation, struggle. The state mustn't turn into the writer's midwife."

He was tremendously amused by the conduct of the Icelandic writer Halldor Laxness, who was awarded the Nobel Prize for Literature this year. Robert has never read anything by him, but he saw a picture in the newspaper that he takes to be characteristic. Robert laughs, remembering Laxness's cockiness during the prize celebration in Stockholm, where he swung the Swedish princess around in a dance. On a path in the woods he shows me how Laxness in his tailcoat twirled her around like a peasant boy, as if crowing: "Now, after winning the East, the West is mine as well!" For shortly before, Laxness had won a prize from the Soviets. In the face of such bravura the little group of German and Swiss Nobel Prize winners shrivels into a bunch of wallflowers.

Here ends my record of our walks together. A few pages from the early days have gotten lost, and I made no notes on our last walks. Did I sense instinctively that the end was near? Did I want to let the traces scatter in silence? I do not know. Brooding over such actions or omissions is pointless. Just as it would be pointless to compose a retouched picture of Robert Walser that does not correspond to reality. To convey his idiosyncratic nature and his opinions truthfully must be my supreme goal; only by fulfilling it can the publication of this intimate portrayal and the forthcoming documentary biography be justified.

If it seems there is much talk of eating and drinking in *Walks with Walser*, if particular themes occasionally repeat in contradictory variations, and if certain parts happen to shock some readers, I have taken these risks in the service of the truth that an original personality like Robert Walser can sustain, even if this casts some shadows upon him. It is a quiet comfort to me that our walks brought a bit of variety into the monotony of his decades of asylum life; I will never again find such a passionate walking companion.

In the twilight of December 25, 1956, I looked out of my dark apartment into the neighborhood, where the first Christmas trees were beginning to twinkle. Next to me lay my sick Dalmatian Ajax, whom on this night I did not want to leave alone. His poor condition had caused me to postpone my next walk with Robert Walser from Christmas to New Year's Day. Suddenly the telephone rang. It brought the news, relayed by the senior doctor, that Robert had been found dead in the early afternoon in a field of snow—just where we had spent unforgettable hours together on Christmas 1954 and Good Friday 1955.

That night I wished to see no more Christmas trees. Their light pained me too deeply.

The Last Walk: Christmas 1956

THE QUIET MORNING of the twenty-fifth of December is followed by the midday meal, which is more lavish than most other days. Robert enjoys his food in the company of his fellow patients; the noise of forks, spoons, and knives, sounds to him like cheerful music. Now, however, he has the urge to walk. Dressed warmly, he steps out into the crystalline light of the snowy landscape. From the asylum, the path leads him through a dim underpass to the train station, where he so often waited for his friend. Soon they will walk together again, on New Year's Day, rain or shine. Now he is drawn up to the Rosenberg, where a ruin stands. He has been there many times, both alone and accompanied. From the ridge, one has an enchanting view of the Alpstein mountain range. The noon hour is so calming: snow, pure snow, as far as the eye can see. Did he not once write a poem that ends with the words: "Snow falls like the limp sparkling of a rose shedding its petals"? The verses weren't particularly good. But it is true, a person should also shed his petals thus: like a rose.

The lonely walker sucks in deep breaths of the clear winter air. One could almost eat it, it's so solid. Herisau now lies under him. Factories, houses, churches, the train station. He climbs the Schochenberg between beeches and firs, perhaps a bit too fast for his age. But he is drawn farther and higher, his heart beating curiously. Up out of the Rosenwald to Wachtenegg, the western tip of the Rosenberg; from there he wants to cross a small hollow to the hill on far side. He is overcome by the desire to light a cigarette. But he does not give in. He saves the pleasure for later, when he reaches the ruin. The descent to the hollow is rather steep. He turns his toes inward and moves carefully step by step, but without grabbing the hedges for support, to the approximately 860-meter dip, where he wants to rest for a few minutes. Only a few more meters and the ground is even again. It must be about half past one now. The sun shines wanly, like a rather anemic young girl. Not victoriously bright, but tenderly melancholic and hesitant, as if today it would like to give the lovely landscape over to night sooner than usual.

Here the heartbeat of the walker suddenly begins to falter. He grows dizzy. A sign of arteriosclerosis due to age, which the doctor once mentioned. Warning him to take a more leisurely pace. In a flash he remembers the leg cramps that plagued him on earlier walks. Will he get cramps now? How irritating such things are, how meddlesome and dumb! There—what is that? He falls suddenly on his back, lifts his right hand to his heart, and lies still. Deathly still. He straightens his left arm to lie against his quickly cooling body. His left hand is balled up, as if the walker wanted to crush the sudden, quick pain that sprung upon him like a panther. His hat lies a bit farther up the hill. His head turned aside, the silent walker now offers the perfect image of Christmas peace. His mouth is open; it is as if the cool, pure winter air is still streaming through him. He is found like this shortly afterwards by two schoolboys, who sledded down from the "Burghalden" farmstead belonging to the Manser family, a mere hundred and fifty meters away, to see who was lying there in the snow. A woman, who climbed out of the valley with her Appenzell mountain dog to pay her father and mother a Christmas visit, said how unusually agitated her "Bläss" had been that morning. Barking loudly, he had kept trying to tear himself from the leash and dash to the slope where something strange and unfamiliar lay. What could it be? Go have a look, boys!

The dead man, who lay on the snowy slope, is a writer, who delighted in winter, with its light, merry dance of snowflakes—a true poet, who longed like a child for a world of quiet, purity, and love:

Robert Walser.